Kenpo Karate Master Keys

The Art of Five Lines and Five Circles

Kenpo Karate Master Keys

The Art of Five Lines and Five Circles

Douglas Parent

ISBN 978-1-7344695-2-3

Library of Congress Control Number: 2020900295

Copyright © 2018 Douglas Parent

All rights reserved. Except for fair use in book reviews, no part of this publication may be reproduced or utilized in any form or by any means, electronic or mechanical, including photocopying, recording, or by an information storage and retrieval system, without prior written permission from the author.

First edition: January 2020

Aqupoint Press, Los Angeles, CA

If you can't teach it then you don't really know it.

This book is dedicated to my instructor,

Mr. Bryan Hawkins

and to the memory of

SGM Edmund K. Parker

Table of Contents

Introduction 1
   Components of Master Key Techniques 3
Kenpo Karate Master Keys 4
   Defining Master Keys 5
   The Master Keys 8
Master Key Moves – Categories 100
Singular Master Key Moves 12
Linear Master Key Moves 18
   Alternating Lines 19
   Parting Lines 27
   Crossing Lines 34
   Opposing Lines 43
   Twin Lines 58
Circular Master Key Moves 70
   Repeating Circles 71
   Following Circles 79
   Spreading Circles 89
   Closing Circles 94
   Reversing Circles 103
End Note 108
Index by Self Defense Technique 110
Index by Belt Level 124

Introduction

Why this book?

During my study of Kenpo Karate, I have heard many arguments both for and against the use of what we term "Self Defense Techniques". Many of these opinions have been wrong either because that person did not really understand how Kenpo is structured or they were unfamiliar with the purpose of using Self Defense Techniques.

This book is an outgrowth of my study of Self Defense Techniques. During my lessons I began to notice how some patterns repeated in various ways. Those of us who practice martial arts have often had a deja-vu type of experience when learning some new move. This is because we've learned a similar motion earlier in our study and we're now applying it in a different situation. As I began to make notes on these motions, I discovered there were five primary linear motions and five primary circular motions. These are all performed using two weapons: two arms, two legs, or one arm and one leg. Both the linear and circular motions contain five sets; each set contains one grouping of sequential moves and four sets of simultaneous moves. There are also a limited group of movements done with a single weapon - arm or leg. I have organized them separately as Singular Techniques.

In the following pages I have attempted to organize the Self Defense Techniques according to their major movements. While each of these "Master Key Techniques" contains multiple movements, I have categorized them into circular, linear and what I term "singular" - meaning they are performed with a single natural weapon such as the hand or leg. For simplicity I have used the term "Master Key Moves" interchangeably with the term "Master Key Techniques". The term Master Key Techniques is technically more accurate, but there could be some confusion with the term "Self Defense Techniques" when discussing concepts. I use the term Master Key Moves which is more commonly recognized in the Kenpo community.

The five common sets of circular and linear moves along with Singular Techniques are the Master Keys of Kenpo. Thus, I have titled this book "Kenpo Karate: The Art of Five Lines and Five Circles".

Some knowledge of Kenpo Karate is useful to understand the concepts presented here.

Background and Self Defense Techniques described in this document were taken from the United Kenpo Systems Self Defense Technique training manual, © 2012; courtesy United Kenpo Systems, Inc.

Introduction

Components of Master Key Techniques

The following definitions are from Ed Parkers "Encyclopedia of Kenpo"; v.1.0, ©1992; Delsby Publications, Pasadena, CA:

Master Key Basic:

a single move that can be used in more than one predicament with equal effect.

Master Key Movements:

Move or series of moves that can be used in more than one predicament. For example, a rear heel kick, shin scrape, and instep stomp can be used for a FULL NELSON, REAR BEAR HUG with the arms free or pinned, REAR ARM LOCK, et. Similarly, an arm break can be applied to a cross wrist grab, a lapel grab, or hair grab - application of the arm break would remain constant, but the methods of controlling the wrist would vary.

Master Key Technique:

The sequence of movements that can be applied to a number of predicaments. See FAMILY RELATED MOVES.

Family Related Moves:

The use of the same move or moves against a number of predicaments that are basically similar in context, but so often overlooked as being similar in principle. For example, the answer to a wrist grab can (via slight alteration) be the same answer to a hair or lapel grab. The basic action is to control the opponent's wrist while striking against the joint of his elbow. The answer to a "rear bear hug", arms free, can also work if the arms were pinned, or if the hug was converted into a "Full Nelson".

Kenpo Karate Master Keys

The Need for Self Defense Techniques

Students of Kenpo karate have many different goals when they begin learning this art. Some enjoy sparring; some may want an interesting workout or they desire to learn how to defend themselves.

Kenpo tests a student in various ways resulting in personal growth, often without them realizing it is happening. However, we must keep in mind that Kenpo is a martial art and our primary reason for learning Kenpo is to become proficient at fighting.

There are four main areas of study within Kenpo that include:

1. Basics: strikes with the natural weapons of the body, blocks, stances, foot maneuvers, etc.
2. Kata: choreographed movement done by an individual to study combinations of basics in motion
3. Sparring: free fighting with opponents in a controlled manner to learn motion and timing
4. Self Defense Techniques: Short choreographed fight sequences with an opponent who initiates a specific attack answered with specific defensive / offensive moves by the defender.

Each of these areas could stand alone as a vehicle for teaching a person to defend himself. It's possible to learn fighting skills just doing Basics by hitting pads and heavy bags. A student might learn the motion of a martial art through kata; or maybe they'll follow the route of some styles where the students spend most of their time sparring with each other.

Each of these contributes value to the learning process but taken individually they offer only a partial solution. To become complete martial artists, we need to study all of these but focus that study with the continual practice of Self Defense Techniques.

Defining Master Keys

Self Defense Techniques are prearranged responses to various attacks. Some may seem repetitive but each instills at least one unique lesson that Mr. Parker intended us to learn. In fact, many of them feature multiple lessons. These are the **Master Keys**; repeating them builds a trained, ingrained response for a particular circumstance. A common name for this response is "muscle memory"; it's not actual memory stored in muscles but rather a way of training one's mind to subconsciously remember the easiest, most efficient method to perform a particular movement. When triggered by an outside stimulus such as a certain type of attack, the subconscious memory helps our body move in an appropriate way.

For those who are unfamiliar with Kenpo Karate or those who are new to the art, the practice of Self Defense Techniques may seem like a waste of time. Technique practice is criticized as an impractical recipe for fighting. 'You couldn't do that in a real fight' is a phrase often used. Unfortunately, these people are missing the main point, that Self Defense Techniques are memory drills. They are designed to make learning Kenpo easier by combining Master Keys into a sequence of moves that can be practiced on another person. We can draw a comparison to kata where martial arts moves are connected in sequence for practice and memorization. Self Defense Techniques are connected in a similar way and then combined with performing these movements on another person.

We continually practice Self Defense Techniques so by the time we reach the rank of Black Belt we have trained our bodies and minds to respond automatically to almost every possible way one person may attack another person. In this manner we learn to spontaneously fight when put into a threatening situation. This is the primary goal in the study of Kenpo Karate.

Master Key patterns of motion contained within the Self Defense Techniques are also seen in other styles of martial arts. They are not unique to Kenpo Karate, but would be recognized by almost any martial artist. There are only so many possible ways a person's body can move, so there is a high level of commonality among the various different arts. Kenpo Karate Master Keys are differentiated by methods used to teach and implement them.

Need for Master Key Moves

Master Key Techniques may contain moves that are both linear and circular. As we perform the Technique a linear move may transition to a circular move and back again. Combinations of these motions are similar in many of the Self Defense Techniques and repeat often. Depending on the situation, one circle may be smaller or larger than a previous instance; one line may be longer or shorter. They are still performed in the same basic pattern even though the circumstances differ. I believe we can improve our skill at Self Defense Techniques by gaining insights via these motion patterns within the Master Key Moves. This will enable us to become more proficient in spontaneous fighting.

Earlier I mentioned the four areas of learning within Kenpo Karate. Aside from study of the Basics, all other areas contribute to our fighting ability. We learn flow and awareness from Kata. Sparring teaches us to be spontaneous with quickness, timing and aggressiveness manner; Self Defense Techniques give us ways to use all of our natural weapons to attack vulnerable targets in a fight. What is often lacking is a way to integrate the lessons we learn from Kata, from Sparring, from Self Defense Techniques.

A good example of this is seen when we compare a Sparring match with a Self Defense Technique line. During the Sparring match the students may exhibit good timing and aggressiveness but only use a limited set of weapons, thus having the appearance of performing basic kickboxing. Meanwhile, during a Technique line, students use many of their natural weapons and attack more vulnerable targets but the timing may be off or the energy is low. It won't look like a "real" fight. Our primary goal in Kenpo Karate is to become expert fighters, if the student only uses basic kickboxing skills in a real engagement then they are not benefiting from their years spent studying Kenpo.

One solution for this problem is to practice sparring using Master Key Basics, Moves and Techniques. For instance, by inserting a Master Key Move when entering an opponent's defenses, the student can use their Kenpo skill as part of a spontaneous fight. They need to practice this during sparring class against varied attacks in order to become proficient with it during a real fight.

The purpose of this book is to define the Master Keys. We may then create practice drills with them to become more proficient. As the Master Keys become internalized a student will naturally go to them for solutions during Sparring practice. When forced into a real fight they will use all the resources available to them as Kenpo Karate martial artists.

The Master Keys

As previously stated, I have categorized the Master Key Moves in linear "Lines", circular "Circles and simple "Singular" sections. What follows is a study of base techniques from Yellow Belt to 1st Black Belt under the Kenpo Karate 16-technique system. Lines and Circles are performed using two weapons, either two arms, two legs, or one of each. Singular techniques are performed using only one weapon, either an arm or a leg. When considering each movement, it is necessary to analyze the intent of that movement. For example, a block may be either linear (thrusting) or circular (hammering); the results of the block determine if the block Master Key is a Line or a Circle.

Notes on Method

- All strikes, whether linear or circular, have a linear effect on the target. They both result in the target moving away in a linear fashion.
- A block is a line; it may be a line of action (example: thrusting inward block) or a path of action (vertical outward block).
- A circular strike cannot cause a circular effect; that can only be caused by a grab or hold with pulling or pushing motion.
- When I describe Master Keys in this book I am primarily talking about combinations of strikes, blocks, checks, parries, etc. Footwork is not described as part of the movements but is important to the effectiveness of these movements. My intent is for the student or instructor to supplement the Master Keys with suggested footwork. In practice, Master Keys may be performed with appropriate, varying stances or foot maneuvers, depending on the lesson goal and the proficiency of the student.
- The "Clock Principle" as used in Kenpo Karate describes angles of attack and defense throughout this book.

Footwork is a fundamental contributor to Kenpo techniques. I consider it extremely important in a person's ability to make their Kenpo effective. A person performing techniques with poor footwork does not truly understand the art of Kenpo Karate. There is no such thing as "arm kenpo". True Kenpo requires a good foundation.

Master Key Moves - Categories

Lines and Circles must use two weapons
two arms, two legs, or one arm and one leg

The Lines: (linear)
1. **Alternating Lines** *sequential*
    a. individual strikes alternate in same direction; on the same plane; left, right punch
2. **Parting Lines** *simultaneous*
    a. different directions, different targets; do not cross each other; Locking Horns
3. **Crossing Lines** *simultaneous*
    a. two weapons cross, different directions; arm bars, Cross of Destruction, Lone Kimono
4. **Opposing Lines** *simultaneous*
    a. push / pull, pull / strike, pull / kick; opposite directions, same plane; B1a
5. **Twin Lines** *simultaneous*
    a. two hands, same direction; pushing, pulling, striking, Begging Hands

The Circles: (circular)
1. **Repeating Circles** *sequential*
    a. follow in same direction; timing varies; double factor; Reversing Mace, Protecting Fans
2. **Following Circles** *simultaneous*
    a. Follow and track; same direction as the same time
3. **Spreading Circles** *simultaneous*
    a. Move in opposite directions outward at same time
4. **Closing Circles** *simultaneous*
    a. Move in opposite directions inward at the same time; sandwich
5. **Reversing Circles** *simultaneous*
    a. Move in opposite directions on reversing paths at the same time

Singular Techniques: single weapon (arm or leg)

Section 1

Linear Master Key Moves

Singular

Section 1

Singular Master Key Moves

YELLOW BELT TECHNIQUES

DELAYED SWORD - (front right-hand lapel grab)

- right inward block; right outward handsword to neck

ALTERNATING MACES – (front two hand push)

- right inward downward block; right outward backnuckle to head

SWORD OF DESTRUCTION - (front left roundhouse punch)

- right outward block; right inward handsword to neck

SWORD AND HAMMER - (right flank left hand shoulder grab)

- right outward handsword to neck; right outward hammer to groin

DEFLECTING HAMMER - (front right thrust kick)

- right outward downward block; right inward elbow to head

CAPTURED TWIGS - (rear high bear hug - arms pinned)

- right downward rear hammer to groin; right upward elbow to chin

Singular Master Key Moves

MACE OF AGGRESSION - (front two hand lapel grab pulling in)

- right straight punch; right inward downward block to arms; right inward elbow to head; right outward elbow to head

ORANGE BELT TECHNIQUES

TRIGGERED SALUTE - (front right-hand direct push)

- right straight heelpalm to chin, right inward hook to arm, right inward elbow to solar plexus, right outward elbow to ribs; right backnuckle to ribs; right uppercut to chin

SHIELDING HAMMER - (front left step thru roundhouse punch)

- right extended outward block; right inward hammer to face; right outward elbow to solar plexus

LONE KIMONO - (front left-hand lapel grab - palm up)

- right lifting thrusting forearm strike to elbow, right inward downward block, right outward handsword

REPEATING MACE - (front left-hand push)

- right inward hammer to kidney, right outward backnuckle to ribs

STRIKING SERPENT'S HEAD - (front bear hug - arms free)

- left inward inverted backnuckle to head; hair pull;

PURPLE BELT TECHNIQUES

CRUSHING HAMMER- (rear high bear hug - arms pinned)

- downward rear hammer to groin, downward rear heelpalm to groin, upward outward elbow to chin

TWISTED TWIG - (front wrist lock)

- upward elbow to chin; outward elbow to solar plexus; downward hammer to groin

BLUE BELT TECHNIQUES

HOOKING WINGS - (front two hand low push)

- right outward hook push, right inward hammer, right outward backnuckle (Figure 8); upward elbow to chin; downward heelpalm to face.

BOW OF COMPULSION - (front wrist lock against opponent's chest)

- upward elbow to chest; downward knuckle rake; upward handsword to groin; outward backnuckle to knee; inward horizontal hook punch to knee

GREEN BELT TECHNIQUES

RETREATING PENDULUM - (front right thrusting heel kick)

- right downward block to kick; right overhead hammer to top of spine;

SNAKING TALON - (front two hand chest push)

- inward hammer to arm; outward handsword to wrist grab (Figure 8); pull

CONQUERING SHIELD - (front left stiff-arm lapel grab)

- upward elbow to elbow; downward elbow to forearm; upward elbow to chin; downward heelpalm to face

3RD DEGREE BROWN BELT TECHNIQUES

CIRCLING THE HORIZON – (front right step thru punch)

- outward, upward backnuckle to face; inward elbow to ribs; downward hammer to knee; inward inverted handsword to groin

GRIPPING TALON – (front left-hand direct wrist grab)

- inward horizontal elbow, outward horizontal elbow, outward backnuckle

BRUSHING THE STORM – (right flank, right step thru overhead club)

- strike down to opponent's solar plexus with inner elbow; underhand heel palm strike to opponent's groin

CIRCLE OF DOOM – (front right straight kick)

- inside, downward (palm down) block; circle arm and execute an extended outward block

DESPERATE FALCONS – (front two-hand grabs to both wrists)

- vertical or diagonal backnuckle strike to temple; inward elbow strike to face; downward hammerfist to kidney
- shoot to a reverse bow to buckle the inside of your opponent's leg; knee strike to the inside of other leg

2nd DEGREE BROWN BELT TECHNIQUES

BROKEN GIFT – (front handshake)

- outward backnuckle strike to temple; inward elbow strike to opposite side jaw

1st DEGREE BLACK BELT TECHNIQUES

ENTWINED MACES – (front right and left punch)

- hand strikes executed in a looping Figure 8 pattern that follows a path and not a line

ESCAPE FROM THE STORM – (right flank overhead club attack)

- inner elbow strike down to opponent's solar plexus; underhand heel palm strike to groin;

Singular Master Key Moves

THRUSTING LANCE – (front right step thru knife thrust)

- underhand stiff-arm lifting back knuckle strike to chin, downward backnuckle strike to nose, inward hammerfist to side of face; Circle and backnuckle to opposite side of face (Figure 8)

CAPTURING THE ROD – (front right pistol against your chest)

- stiff arm lifting backnuckle strike to side of jaw; reverse your motion and Figure 8 strikes to jaw;

FATAL DEVIATION – (front right punch and left punch with opponent's left leg forward)

- inward horizontal elbow strike to jaw; back hammerfist to groin

ENTWINED LANCE – (front right step thru knife thrust)

- upward flapping elbow strike under chin; outward backnuckle strike to jaw hinge

BROKEN ROD – (rear right hand pistol)

- vertical lifting upward strike under chin, diagonal downward strike to temple, loop and outward downward hammer strike to elbow; inward upward rake to lower ribcage; diagonal outward downward strike to back of neck; upward diagonal strike to side of face

DEFYING THE ROD – (front right pistol hold-up)

- inward strike to opponent's bicep, then forearm; right upward flapping elbow strike under chin; diagonal outward downward strike to back of neck

Section 2

Linear Master Key Moves

The Lines

2.1

Alternating Lines

YELLOW BELT TECHNIQUES

ATTACKING MACE - (straight right punch to face)

- execute a right straight thrust punch to the right lower rib cage of your opponent; left snapping vertical punch to your opponent's right kidney

CHECKING THE STORM - (right overhead club attack)

- left front snapping ball kick to your opponent's groin; right snapping knife-edge kick to the inside of your opponent's right knee

ORANGE BELT TECHNIQUES

THRUSTING SALUTE - (front right step-through kick)

- right front snap ball kick to opponent's groin; right torqueing heel palm strike to opponent's chin;

FIVE SWORDS - (front right step through roundhouse punch)

- right outward handsword to neck; left five-finger thrust to eyes; right uppercut punch to solar plexus; left outward handsword strike to neck

EVADING THE STORM - (right front step through overhead club attack)

- left (clenched) horizontal punch; left knee strike to the outside of your opponent's right thigh; right roundhouse knee strike to the inside of your opponent's right thigh

CLUTCHING FEATHERS - (front left-hand hair grab)

- pin your opponent's left hand to your head with your left hand as you thrust a right vertical middle-knuckle fist to your opponent's left armpit; left thrusting heel palm strike to your opponent's jaw

STRIKING SERPENT'S HEAD - (front bear hug - arms free)

- left hand grab and pull your opponent's hair back while executing a right snapping half fist to your opponent's throat.

PURPLE BELT TECHNIQUES

LEAPING CRANE - (front right step through punch)

- right snapping knife-edge kick to the outside of your opponent's right knee; right outward back knuckle strike to your opponent's left kidney

OBSCURE SWORD - (right flank left hand shoulder grab)

- right outward handsword to your opponent's throat; left front snap ball kick to your opponent's groin

BUCKLING BRANCH - (front left step through straight kick)

- right front snap ball kick to your opponent's groin; left knife-edge kick to the inside and back of your opponent's right knee

BLUE BELT TECHNIQUES

PARTING WINGS - (front two-hand push)

- right thrusting inward handsword to your opponent's left lower ribcage; left outward handsword to your opponent's throat; right vertical middle knuckle punch into your opponent's solar plexus

DARTING MACE - (front two-hand grab to the right wrist)

- left vertical punch to your opponent's chin; right vertical punch to your opponent's solar plexus; thrusting outward handsword strike to your opponent's throat; right heel palm strike to your opponent's chin

CHARGING RAM - (front tackle with your opponent's arms extended)

- snap a right front ball kick to your opponent's left ribcage; left roundhouse kick to your opponent's face

THUNDERING HAMMERS - (front right step through punch)

- left inward block at or above the outside of your opponent's right elbow; right inward horizontal forearm strike across opponent's stomach,

GREEN BELT TECHNIQUES

BEGGING HANDS - (front two-hand grab to wrists)

- right front snapping ball kick to your opponent's groin; left front snapping ball kick to your opponent's chin or chest;

3rd DEGREE BROWN BELT TECHNIQUES

DETOUR FROM DOOM - (front right roundhouse kick)

- right vertical punch to your opponent's face; right front snapping ball kick to your opponent's groin; left vertical punch to your opponent's solar plexus

RETURNING STORM - (right roundhouse and backhand club attack)

- front snapping ball kick to your opponent's right ribcage; right upward lifting stiff-arm back knuckle strike to your opponent's face

GLANCING SPEAR - (front right direct wrist grab to left arm)

- left outward elbow strike to your opponent's right lower ribcage; right horizontal finger thrust to his eyes

ENCOUNTER WITH DANGER - (front two-hand push)

- left vertical knife-edge kick to your opponent's groin; knife-edge kick under your opponent's jaw; left back thrusting heel kick to your opponent's stomach

CIRCLING DESTRUCTION - (left step through punch)

- left inward horizontal heel palm strike to your opponent's face; right inward hand sword to the right side of your opponent's neck

2nd DEGREE BROWN BELT TECHNIQUES

ESCAPE FROM DEATH - (right rear-arm choke)

- right heel palm strike to your opponent's chin; right knee strike to the outside of your opponent's thigh

1st DEGREE BROWN BELT TECHNIQUES

CIRCLING FANS - (front left / right punch combination)

- front snapping ball kick to your opponent's groin; thrust a right upper cut punch to your opponent's forehead; left vertical punch to your opponent's sternum; right knee into your opponent's groin

DANCE OF DARKNESS - (front right kick and right punch combination)

- right two-finger hook to your opponent's left eye; left two-finger eye poke to your opponent's left eye
- right "retarded ball kick" to your opponent's jaw; left side thrusting knife-edge kick to your opponent's face.

CLIPPING THE STORM - (front right thrusting club)

- left inward downward handsword to the outside of your opponent's right forearm; right downward handsword strike to the outside of your opponent's right wrist
- outward handsword (palm down) to your opponent's throat; right thrusting heel palm strike under your opponent's chin

PARTING OF THE SNAKES - (front right punch / rear attempt)

- left front snapping ball kick to his solar plexus/front right snapping ball kick to his chin (chicken); thrusting heel palm strike to the chin; right back snapping heel kick/left back snapping heel kick to any available openings

THRUST INTO DARKNESS - (rear right step through punch)

- left thrusting back heel kick to your opponent's stomach; right front snapping ball kick to your opponent's chest; right knife-edge kick to the outside of his right knee

FATAL CROSS - (front two-hand attempted low grab or push)

- left step through knee kick to your opponent's groin; right step through knee kick to his solar plexus
- right knee to his lower spine; left knee kick to your opponent's right kidney

COURTING THE TIGER - (flank left and right arm & shoulder grab / two men)

- left foot kicks his right lower ribs; right foot kicks him in the sternum

GATHERING OF THE SNAKES - (front left / rear right punch / two men)

- left inward horizontal heel palm strike to your opponent's face; right inward hand sword to the right side of your opponent's neck

GLANCING LANCE - (front right shuffle knife thrust)

- right front snap ball kick to your opponent's groin; right two-finger inward hook to your opponent's eyes.

1st DEGREE BLACK BELT TECHNIQUES

RAM AND THE EAGLE - (front right punch and rear left hand collar grab)

- right front snap ball kick to the groin; strike to the right side of your opponent's neck with a right outward hand sword; left five-finger thrust (palm down) to your opponent's eyes; right uppercut punch to your opponent's stomach; left outward handsword strikes to the left side of your opponent's neck

THRUSTING LANCE - (front right step-through low knife thrust)

- front chicken kick

REPRIMANDING THE BEARS - (front right punch and rear bear hug, arms pinned)

- left knife edge kick to the sternum; left outward back knuckle strike to the head; right thrusting ball kick to the sternum

2.2
Parting Lines

ORANGE BELT TECHNIQUES

LOCKING HORNS - (front headlock)

- right underhand reverse handsword to your opponent's groin with a left-hand check (strike) just above your opponent's right knee

PURPLE BELT TECHNIQUES

CALMING THE STORM - (front right step through roundhouse club)

- left extended outward block to the inside of your opponent's right arm with a right vertical punch to your opponent's jaw

TWISTED TWIG - (front wrist lock)

- the inside of your opponent's right knee with your right knee as you deliver a right upward elbow strike to your opponent's solar plexus and/or jaw

BLUE BELT TECHNIQUES

SQUEEZING THE PEACH - (rear bear hug - arms pinned)

- buckle your opponent's left inner knee by stomping into a right reverse bow toward 7:30 and execute a right obscure back elbow strike to the chin

GREEN BELT TECHNIQUES

SHIELD AND MACE - (front right step through punch)

- right vertical outward block to the outside of your opponent's right arm with a straight punch to your opponent's right lower ribcage

FLASHING WINGS - (front right step through punch)

- left hand slides down and past your opponent's right shoulder to check and pin his right arm to his body. Simultaneously with this action execute a right upward thrusting hand sword (palm up) to your opponent's throat.

3rd DEGREE BROWN BELT TECHNIQUES

DETOUR FROM DOOM - (front right roundhouse kick)

- left downward block to the inside of your opponent's right leg as you thrust a right vertical punch to your opponent's face

Linear Master Key Moves

GRIPPING TALON - (front left-hand direct wrist grab)

- right reverse bow to buckle the inside of your opponent's left leg as you a right looping inner diagonal wrist strike to the right side of your opponent's neck

BROKEN RAM - (front tackle with your opponent's arms wide)

- strike to your opponent's left jaw hinge with a right downward hammerfist as you shoot into your right reverse bow to buckle his leg

2nd DEGREE BROWN BELT TECHNIQUES

ESCAPE FROM DEATH - (right rear-arm choke)

- right hand simultaneously grab and pull down on your opponent's right wrist as you deliver a left back elbow strike to your opponent's solar plexus

MENACING TWIRL - (left hand rear belt grab)

- deliver a right outside downward block to the inside of your opponent's left (grabbing) arm at the wrist. Synchronize a left thrusting heel palm strike to your opponent's chin

SECURING THE STORM - (front right step through roundhouse club)

- left extended outward block to the inside of your opponent's right wrist. Simultaneously deliver a right vertical punch to your opponent's face.

1st DEGREE BROWN BELT TECHNIQUES

BEAR AND THE RAM - (front right punch / rear bear hug, arms free)

- right inward block to the inside of the right arm with a right front thrusting ball kick to the groin

GRASPING EAGLES - (front right lapel grab / rear right shoulder grab)

- right front snap ball kick to the groin simultaneous with a left inward vertical forearm strike to the outside of the right elbow of your front opponent (opponent #1). While employing these dual strikes to your front opponent, deliver a right back thrusting hammerfist strike to the groin of your rear opponent
- right thrusting heel palm strike to opponent #1's chin. Simultaneous with this heel palm, deliver a left underhand heel palm strike to the chin of opponent #2.

PARTING OF THE SNAKES - (front right punch / rear attempt)

- right back thrusting heel kick to the solar plexus of your aggressively charging rear opponent (opponent #2) while simultaneously deliver a right thrusting vertical punch to the face of opponent #1

UNFURLING CRANE - (front left and right punch)

- under his jaw with a right obscure elbow. Continue your Path of

Travel and transform it into an upward five-finger claw to your opponent's face as you execute a left thrusting heel palm strike to your opponent's solar plexus, and a right front scoop kick to his groin.

CIRCLING WINDMILLS - (front two-hand push followed by a right-hand punch)

- right upward / right extended outward block to the outside of your opponent's right arm as you execute a left heel palm strike to your opponent's solar plexus

REVERSING CIRCLES - (front left roundhouse kick and left punch combo)

- right upward block under, as well as inside of, his left attacking arm. Simultaneous with your right block deliver a left thrusting heel palm (fingers pointing toward 3 o'clock) to his left floating ribs.

UNWINDING PENDULUM - (front right kick and right punch combination)

- right reverse bow to buckle the inside of his right leg as you execute a right outward heel palm claw strike to your opponent's left kidney
- shoot back into a left reverse bow to buckle the inside of your opponent's left knee. As you execute a left elbow strike to the back of your opponent's head

1st DEGREE BLACK BELT TECHNIQUES

ENTWINED MACES - (front left and right punch combination)

- shoot into a right reverse bow as you buckle the inside of your opponent's left knee. Simultaneous with the buckle deliver a right downward hammerfist to your opponent's groin

RAM AND THE EAGLE - (front right punch and rear left hand collar grab)

- left inward block to the outside of opponent #1's right punch. Simultaneous with this action deliver a right over the shoulder back knuckle strike to the bridge of the nose of opponent #2.

CAPTURING THE ROD - (front right pistol against your chest)

- have your right hand yank the gun from your opponent's grip. Have the gun travel back, toward, and past your right hip (with your left hand still checking the pistol hand) while simultaneously executing a right front snap ball kick to your opponent's groin.

FATAL DEVIATION - (front right and left punch combination)

- right extended outward block to the inside of your opponent's left punching arm. Simultaneous with your shuffle and block, execute a left thrusting vertical punch to your opponent's face.
- shoot into a right reverse bow to further buckle the inside of your opponent's right leg and expose his groin while executing a right back hammerfist to your opponent's groin.

Linear Master Key Moves

REPRIMANDING THE BEARS - (front right punch and rear bear hug, arms pinned)

- shoot to a right reverse bow to purposely buckle opponent's left leg simultaneous with a right downward heel palm strike to the groin

ENTWINED LANCE - (front right step-through knife thrust - low)

- have your right hand travel as a sliding check down your opponent's right arm to control his right wrist as you simultaneously deliver a left two-finger eye poke to your opponent's eyes

PIERCING LANCE - (front right low knife thrust while arms are up)

- pivot to a neutral bow and buckle your opponent's right leg while simultaneously executing a right back elbow strike to your opponent's right or left ribcage

UNFOLDING THE DARK - (right rear flank left step-through punch)

- left spinning stiff-leg sweep to the outside of your opponent's left leg and pivot info a left neutral bow as you simultaneously deliver a left outward backnuckle strike to your opponent's left kidney.

2.3

Crossing Lines

YELLOW BELT TECHNIQUES

THE GRASP OF DEATH - (side headlock)

- simultaneously strike the back of your opponent's right elbow with your left forearm while pulling in and toward you with your right hand (arm bar)

ORANGE BELT TECHNIQUES

LONE KIMONO - (front left-hand lapel grab)

- pin your opponent's left hand to your chest, as you deliver a right upward forearm strike against his left elbow

GIFT OF DESTRUCTION - (handshake)

- right hand JERKS your opponent's right hand toward you diagonally and down past your right hip as you strike in and against the joint of your opponent's right elbow with your left heel palm

GLANCING SALUTE - (front right-hand cross push)

- right arm pins your opponent's right wrist to the right side of your chest along with the execution of a left inward vertical forearm strike against the joint of your opponent's right elbow

PURPLE BELT TECHNIQUES

SNAPPING TWIG - (front left-hand chest push)

- right hooking inward horizontal heel palm strike to the outside of your opponent's left elbow along with a left inward horizontal heel palm strike to the inside of your opponent's left wrist

CROSSING TALON - (front right cross wrist grab)

- grab his right wrist with your right hand as you strike your opponent's right elbow with a left inward vertical forearm, while your right hand pulls in, toward, and past your right hip. (arm bar)

LOCKED WING - (rear hammerlock)

- right hand counter grabs your opponent's right wrist as you strike the back of your opponent's right elbow with the inner portion of your left elbow

CALMING THE STORM - (front right step through roundhouse club)

- left vertical punch to your opponent's solar plexus as your right hand frictionally slides down your opponent's right arm, as it acts as a check

BLUE BELT TECHNIQUES

OBSTRUCTING THE STORM - (front right step through overhead club)

- Grab your opponent's right wrist with your right hand as you simultaneously strike your opponent's right elbow with your left

- forearm by first thrusting vertically and then rolling it horizontally forcing your opponent's right arm down while your right hand pulls in, down, and past your right hip. (thrusting arm bar)

TWIN KIMONO - (front two-hand lapel grab pushing out)

- left arm pins your opponent's arms at the wrists as you deliver a right upward forearm strike against your opponent's elbow joints

CROSS OF DESTRUCTION - (rear two-hand choke)

- have your left hand cross your opponent's left arm over his own right arm and break his elbow

FLIGHT TO FREEDOM - (rear hammerlock)

- right hand grabs your opponent's right wrist and twist your opponent's right arm clockwise (in a very tight circle) as your left hand positionally checks (or heel palms)

GREEN BELT TECHNIQUES

CONQUERING SHIELD - (front left stiff-arm lapel grab)

- Pin your opponent's left grabbing hand to your chest with your left hand as you execute a right inward vertical forearm strike against your opponent's left elbow

WINGS OF SILK - (rear two-arm lock)

- pin your opponent's left arm against your stomach or waist with your left hand and arm as you deliver an uppercut forearm break to your opponent's left elbow joint

Linear Master Key Moves

ENTANGLED WING - (front arm lock as instructed)

- have your right arm pull your opponent's left arm down and toward you, positioning it at the elbow and break it across the top of your shoulder

3rd DEGREE BROWN BELT TECHNIQUES

RETURNING STORM - (right roundhouse and backhand club attack)

- grab your opponent's right wrist with your right hand while pushing out with your left forearm (arm bar)

FALLEN CROSS - (rear two-hand choke)

- have both of your arms force your opponent's arms down even further. Meet this action with the right knee up and against the left elbow joint of your opponent

OBSCURE CLAWS - (right flank left hand shoulder grab)

- use your left hand to pin your opponent's left hand to your right shoulder as you deliver a right uppercut forearm strike against the elbow joint of your opponent's left arm

TWIST OF FATE - (front two-hand push)

- twist your opponent's arms and cross them counterclockwise over your left shoulder

GIFT OF DESTINY - (front handshake)

- at the completion of your right-hand twist reach further around your opponent's right wrist with your left hand, this allows you to twist your opponent's wrist even further. As you settle into your left neutral bow release your right hand and chamber it. Immediately execute a right heel palm thrust strike to the back of your opponent's right hand

SQUATTING SACRIFICE - (rear bear hug - arms free)

- both of your elbows strike down to your opponent's forearms. Have both of your hands grab and pull up on your opponent's right ankle to force him on his back. The pulling and squatting could cause your opponent's knee to break

BROKEN RAM - (front tackle with your opponent's arms wide)

- With your opponent's left arm attempting to grasp your waist, pivot to your left into a right reverse bow and deliver a right uppercut forearm strike against the joint of your opponent's left elbow

2nd DEGREE BROWN BELT TECHNIQUES

CAPTURING THE STORM - (front right step through overhead club)

- your right hand forces the club out of your opponent's grasp by fulcruming the action against your opponent's thumb;

Linear Master Key Moves

- have your right arm loop counterclockwise and have the club, that you now control, strike to the back of your opponent's right elbow.

SECURING THE STORM - (front right step through roundhouse club)

- deliver a left uppercut forearm strike over and under your opponent's left arm to break the elbow

FALLING FALCON - (front right direct lapel grab)

- have your right hand grab your opponent's right wrist, and twist it clockwise, applying great pressure on his right wrist and shoulder. Simultaneous with these actions deliver a left underhand heel palm strike to your opponent's right elbow
- while still maintaining your left-hand grab, utilize the residual torque of your pivot to deliver a right kick using the right side of your shin to strike the back of your opponent's right elbow

BOWING TO BUDDHA - (front - right roundhouse kick)

- left inward elbow strike to your opponent's solar plexus. While striking, have your right-hand counter manipulate your opponent's left leg. This action involves a jerk and pull with your right hand, combined with a strikedown with your left elbow
- have your right leg shoot against the underside of your opponent's left leg – specifically the knee. Simultaneously have both of your hands push down (toward 6 o'clock) on top of your opponent's left foot to force, lock, overextend, and fracture his left knee.

GLANCING WING - (front left uppercut punch)

- simultaneously deliver a right inward diagonal block to the outside of your opponent's left uppercut while delivering a left vertical punch to your opponent's face

1st DEGREE BROWN BELT TECHNIQUES

LEAP OF DEATH - (front right step-through straight punch)

- have your right hand grab your opponent's right wrist while delivering a left inward horizontal heel palm strike under and to the outside of your opponent's right elbow.
- maintain control of your opponent's right wrist, while simultaneously delivering a left inward heel palm strike to the back of his right shoulder.

REVERSING CIRCLES - (front left roundhouse kick and left punch combo)

- while grabbing your opponent's left wrist deliver a right downward forearm strike to your opponent's left elbow while simultaneously pulling up with your left hand

GLANCING LANCE - (front right shuffle knife thrust)

- grab his right wrist with your right hand and simultaneously deliver a left inward horizontal heel palm strike to the outside of his right elbow

1st DEGREE BLACK BELT TECHNIQUES

DESTRUCTIVE KNEEL - (front right step-through punch)

- have your right hand grab your opponent's right wrist, twist his arm clockwise (at the wrist), to properly align your opponent's right elbow, and deliver a left inward diagonal heel palm strike to your opponent's right elbow.

SCAPE FROM THE STORM - (right flank, right overhead club attack)

- while controlling your opponent's right hip and leg with your hands, execute a right front crossover toward 7:30 into a low right front twist stance. As you settle into your twist stance, drop your opponent's right knee across your right knee.

THRUSTING LANCE - (front right step-through low knife thrust)

- have your right-hand hook over (shape of a crane) and under your opponent's right elbow. Simultaneous with this action, execute a left vertical elbow strike to the underside of your opponent's armpit

CIRCLING THE STORM - (front right club thrust)

- have your left hand rip across your opponent's face with a left outward claw. With your opponent falling back and toward you execute a right upward lifting forearm strike to the back of his neck.

Kenpo Karate Master Keys

PIERCING LANCE - (front right low knife thrust while arms are up)

- while pulling your opponent down with both of your hands. Guide and force your opponent's right elbow onto your left knee with all intentions of causing an arm break.
- your left hand twists your opponent's right hand clockwise to possibly sprain or break his wrist, simultaneously wrap your opponent's left arm around your left leg. Continue to have your left hand rotate clockwise (if the clock is to your left) and toward you while simultaneously pushing down on your opponent's outer right elbow with your right heel palm to cause your opponent's right shoulder to dislocate.
- twist your opponent's right arm clockwise to place greater pressure on his left wrist and shoulder. Simultaneous with the twist have your left heel palm strike your opponent's right elbow to cause a possible sprain or break.

2.4
Opposing Lines

YELLOW BELT TECHNIQUES

ATTACKING MACE - (straight right punch to face)

- pull your opponent's arm diagonally down past your right hip while simultaneously delivering a right roundhouse kick to his groin.

SWORD AND HAMMER - (right shoulder grab)

- striking your opponent's throat with a right outward handsword. Simultaneous with this action pin your opponent's left hand to your right shoulder with your left hand

MACE OF AGGRESSION - (two hand lapel grab)

- simultaneously strike diagonally through the bridge of your opponent's nose (toward 10:30) with a right inward, downward raking back knuckle strike. Have your left hand pin and check both of your opponent's hands to your chest at the same time the stomp and strike are taking place.

ORANGE BELT TECHNIQUES

TRIGGERED SALUTE - (front right-hand direct push)

- thrust a right heel palm strike to your opponent's chin, as your left hand pins and checks your opponent's right hand to your chest.

EVADING THE STORM - (right front step through overhead club attack)

- left (clenched) horizontal punch to your opponent's right kidney while having your right hand pull your opponent's right arm down and past your right hip.

GIFT OF DESTRUCTION - (handshake)

- your right hand jerks your opponent's right hand toward you diagonally and down past your right hip as you deliver a right knee kick to your opponent's groin

CLUTCHING FEATHERS - (front left-hand hair grab)

- pin your opponent's left hand to your head with your left hand as you thrust a right vertical middle-knuckle fist to your opponent's left armpit.

GLANCING SALUTE - (front right-hand cross push)

- your right hand pulls your opponent's head down and toward the ground (anchoring your right elbow in the process) while executing a right knee strike to your opponent's stomach.

ANCE OF DEATH - (front right straight punch with left leg forward)

- right inward horizontal elbow strike to your opponent's right lower rib cage as your left hand contours down the right side of

- your opponent's body, slides along his right leg, grabs the back of your opponent's right knee, and then pulls toward you, so that your left hand grab concludes at your opponent's right ankle

PURPLE BELT TECHNIQUES

OBSCURE WING - (right flank left hand shoulder grab)

- deliver a right back elbow strike to your opponent's solar plexus as your left hand pins and checks your opponent's left hand to your right shoulder.

SNAPPING TWIG - (front left-hand chest push)

- have your right hand (while forming the shape of a crane) hook over the top of your opponent's left arm, then frictionally pull (yank) your opponent's left arm down and past your right hip, while thrusting left outward handsword strike (palm down and thumb toward you) to your opponent's throat

SPIRALING TWIG - (rear bear hug - arms free)

- right front snapping ball kick to the right ribs of your opponent, while continuing to pull your opponent's right arm past your right hip

CRUSHING HAMMER - (rear bear hug - arms pinned)

- strike your opponent's groin with a right back hammerfist as you pin your opponent's left arm to you with your left hand.

LOCKED WING - (rear hammerlock)

- hand counter grabs your opponent's right wrist while you deliver a left outward elbow strike to your opponent's jaw.

CAPTURED LEAVES - (right flank finger lock)

- raise your right hand high and deliver a left back elbow strike to the back of your opponent's left kidney

BLUE BELT TECHNIQUES

OBSTRUCTING THE STORM - (front right step through overhead club)

- while your right hand pulls his arm in, down, and past your right hip deliver a right snapping knee strike to your opponent's head or chest.

DARTING MACE - (front two-hand grab to the right wrist)

- your right hand counter grabs and pulls your opponent's right wrist, left vertical punch to your opponent's chin

CIRCLING WING – (rear two-hand choke)

- right elbow circles over and down to pin opponent's arm; left four-finger thrust to eyes

GIFT IN RETURN - (front hand shake)

- grab your opponent's right wrist pull and lift with your left hand as you push down against your opponent's right hip with your right hand

FLIGHT TO FREEDOM - (rear hammerlock)

- grab to your opponent's right wrist, pulling your opponent to you as you deliver a right thrusting back heel kick, to your opponent's right ribcage

GREEN BELT TECHNIQUES

THRUSTING WEDGE - (front two-hand high push)

- right upward elbow strike under your opponent's chin as your left arm and hand slide down your opponent's right arm to his right wrist (frictional pull), grab his right wrist and jerk that arm down, past and below your left hip

RAKING MACE - (front two-hand lapel grab - pull in)

- simultaneously execute a right uppercut punch to your opponent's solar plexus and pin both of your opponent's hands horizontally to your chest with your left hand

DESTRUCTIVE TWINS - (two-hand choke - pull in)

- deliver a right straight thrust punch to your opponent's ribcage; simultaneously have your left hand grab the upper portion of your opponent's left arm, slide down to his left wrist, then grab and pull it diagonally down and past your left hip

DEFYING THE STORM - (front right step through roundhouse club)

- have your left hand grab your opponent's right wrist and have your right hand grab the back of your opponent's right elbow; push his right wrist out and away from you while pulling and rolling his right elbow down and toward you

TRIPPING ARROW - (rear bear hug - arms free)

- trip your opponent over your right leg with a right heel palm strike to the jaw
- left hand grab your opponent's right wrist and pull as you thrust a right heel stomp under your opponent's chin

SNAKING TALON - (front two-hand push)

- have your right hand pull your opponent's right arm toward you, down and to your right as you deliver a right front snapping ball kick to your opponent's groin.

Linear Master Key Moves

REPEATED DEVASTATION - (full nelson)

- right outward thrusting elbow strike to the right side of your opponent's jaw and pin your opponent's left forearm to your body with your left forearm.
- left outward thrusting elbow strike to the left side of your opponent's jaw. During this action have your right forearm maintain a check

3rd DEGREE BROWN BELT TECHNIQUES

GRIPPING TALON - (front left-hand direct wrist grab)

- circle your left hand counterclockwise, counter grabbing your opponent's left wrist (pulling it down and past your left hip) as you deliver a right downward hammerfist to your opponent's groin

CIRCLING DESTRUCTION - (front left step through punch)

- deliver a right front scoop kick to your opponent's groin (from behind). Simultaneously with this motion thrust a left outward heel palm strike to your opponent's left kidney with a right two-finger eye hook to his right eye.

BRUSHING THE STORM - (right flank, right step through overhead club)

- have your right hand pull your opponent's right leg toward you (sliding your hand to his right knee cap and to a level below that point). Simultaneously have your left hand push forward at your opponent's right hip.

DOMINATING CIRCLES - (front offset right hand grab to right shoulder)

- rotate into a reverse bow that trips your opponent as you deliver a right thrusting heel palm strike to the right side of your opponent's mandible.

SQUATTING SACRIFICE - (rear bear hug - arms free)

- grab on your opponent's right ankle with your right hand and have your left hand grab your opponent's left wrist. Pull and jerk up with both of your arms as your right foot stomps to the lower spine

2nd DEGREE BROWN BELT TECHNIQUES

CIRCLES OF PROTECTION - (front right step through overhead punch)

- deliver a left outward back knuckle strike to your opponent's face as your right hand grabs and pulls your opponent's testicles

Linear Master Key Moves

BROKEN GIFT - (front handshake)

- right outward back knuckle strike to your opponent's right temple as you retain your left grab on your opponent's right wrist, pulling your opponent's right arm toward you

CROSS OF DEATH - (front two-hand cross choke)

- have your left hand pin your opponent's hands to your chest and deliver a right glancing inward vertical forearm strike against your opponent's left elbow to break it.

SECURING THE STORM - (front right step-through roundhouse club)

- circle your right foot, immediately thrust it toward 6 o'clock into a left forward bow as you simultaneously thrust your right heel palm strike to your opponent's jaw

HEAVENLY ASCENT - (front two-hand choke, arms straight)

- deliver a right half-fist uppercut strike to your opponent's throat; simultaneously have your left hand slide down your opponent's right arm, grabbing your opponent's right wrist and pulling it past your left ribcage

FALLING FALCON - (front right direct lapel grab)

- left hand pin your opponent's right grabbing hand to your chest. Simultaneously with these actions, deliver a right upward elbow strike to your opponent's right shoulder at the head of the humerus.

TAMING THE MACE - (front right step-through punch with a wall behind you)

- left hand check and grab your opponent's right hand at the wrist as you deliver a right outward back knuckle strike to your opponent's right temple

BOWING TO BUDDHA - (front right roundhouse kick)

- left inward elbow strike to your opponent's solar plexus while you jerk and pull with your right hand, combined with a strikedown with your left elbow

1st DEGREE BROWN BELT TECHNIQUES

DANCE OF DARKNESS - (front right kick and right punch combination)

- left hand grab your opponent's right shoulder. As you firmly pull down on your opponent's right shoulder (to control his Height Zones) simultaneously thrust a right vertical back knuckle strike to your opponent's right temple.
- left front crossover sweep (toward 4:30) to your opponent's right leg as you execute a right two-finger hook to your opponent's left eye

Linear Master Key Moves

FALCONS OF FORCE - (flank left and right shoulder grabs / two men)

- pin your opponent's left hand with your left hand. Simultaneous with this pin execute a right outward handsword to his throat.
- your right hand checks the right hand of opponent. Without pause in your action, pivot counterclockwise into a left neutral bow (facing 7:30) as your left hand executes a left outward handsword to the throat

PROTECTING FANS - (front left and right punch combination)

- execute a horizontal finger thrust to your opponent's eyes as you deliver a right front snapping ball kick to his groin while grabbing and pulling his right arm diagonally down past your hip.
- right front scoop kick to your opponent's groin, closely followed by a right two-finger hook to his eyes with a thrusting heel palm strike to his sternum

LEAP OF DEATH - (front right step-through straight punch)

- maintain control of your opponent's right wrist with your right hand while simultaneously delivering a left outward back knuckle strike to your opponents' right lower ribcage

CIRCLING WINDMILLS - (front two-hand push followed by a right-hand punch)

- right front crossover foot sweep (toward 7:30) to the inside of your opponent's right foot as you execute a left inward horizontal finger slice to your opponent's eyes

- left hand grab your opponent's right wrist to counter manipulate him while simultaneously executing a right thrusting heel palm strike to his chin
- left hand still maintaining its grab to your opponent's right wrist as you execute a right underhand stiff-arm back knuckle strike to your opponent's face

GATHERING OF THE SNAKES - (front left / rear right punch / two men)

- grab his shoulders and deliver a right knife-edge kick to the back of opponent's left knee. As you kick, counter balance your kick by pulling your arms toward you

DESTRUCTIVE FANS - (left flank right step-through punch)

- right foot step back toward 3 o'clock into a left forward bow, buckling the back of your opponent's right leg with your calf meeting his calf. With your opponent falling toward the ground, execute a right uppercut punch to his head simultaneous with the sweep

1st DEGREE BLACK BELT TECHNIQUES

DESTRUCTIVE KNEEL - (front right step-through punch)

- left hand (in the shape of a crane) hooks around and to the right, as well as to the front of, your opponent's neck; anchor your left elbow down (using your opponent's right shoulder and back as a fulcrum to leverage your action) to force your opponent back and toward you. This action is simultaneously executed with a left knee strike to your opponent's spine

ENTWINED MACES - (front left & right front punch combination)

- grab your opponent's right wrist. Immediately push-drag forward, pivot into a right forward bow, and deliver a left vertical punch to your opponent's face while pulling your opponent's right arm diagonally down and past your right hip.

ESCAPE FROM THE STORM - (right flank right overhead club attack)

- right hand pulls your opponent's right leg toward you (sliding your hand to his right knee cap and to a level below that point) while simultaneously having your left hand push forward on your opponent's right hip

THRUSTING LANCE - (front right step-through low knife thrust)

- your right hand grabs your opponent's right wrist as you deliver a left underhand heel palm strike and grab your opponent's groin

CAPTURING THE ROD - (front right pistol - against your chest)

- have your right hand yank the gun from your opponent's grip. Have the gun travel back, toward, and past your right hip (with your left hand still checking the pistol hand) while simultaneously executing a right front snap ball kick to your opponent's groin.

REPRIMANDING THE BEARS - (front right punch and rear bear hug, arms pinned)

- execute a right front thrusting ball kick to the groin of opponent #1 while simultaneously executing a right back hammerfist to the groin of opponent #2
- grab, pull, and force his head down while simultaneously delivering a right knee kick to his face

CIRCLING THE STORM - (front - right club thrust)

- left hand circles counterclockwise, up, around, and to the right side of your opponent's face to grab his head at the jaw. As you pull your opponent's head back follow up with a right knee kick to his mid-spine

ENTWINED LANCE - (front right step-through low knife thrust)

- right knee buckles the inside of your opponent's right knee as you deliver a right thrusting heel palm strike to the right side of your opponent's jaw; simultaneous with the buckle and heel palm, have your left hand grab your opponent's right wrist
- left hand grab of your opponent's right wrist while simultaneously executing a right outward back knuckle strike to your opponent's right lower ribcage.

Linear Master Key Moves

BROKEN ROD - (right rear hand pistol against your back)

- have your right hand grab your opponent's right hand including the pistol while simultaneously executing a left uppercut strike to the underside of your opponent's left elbow
- have your left hand gravitationally check your opponent's right shoulder while yanking the pistol out of your opponent's right hand with your right hand

PIERCING LANCE - (front right low knife thrust while arms are up)

- Cock your left leg and deliver a left heel stomp to the right side of your opponent's neck. This is done as both of your hands grab and pull up

DEFYING THE ROD - (front right pistol)

- grab to your opponent's right hand (at the pistol), as you execute a right front snapping ball kick to your opponent's groin simultaneous with a right two-finger eye poke to your opponent's eyes

2.5

Twin Lines

ORANGE BELT TECHNIQUES

FIVE SWORDS - (front right step-through roundhouse punch)

- right inward block to the inside of your opponent's right forearm, while your left hand checks high at your opponent's wrist

CRASHING WINGS - (rear bear hug - arms free)

- strike down with both of your elbows against your opponent's forearms

SCRAPING HOOF - (full nelson)

- thrust both of your fists toward the ground (to help free you from your opponent's grasp, and to pin his arms to your body

PURPLE BELT TECHNIQUES

SPIRALING TWIG - (rear bear hug - arms free)

- your right and left middle knuckle fists strike to the back of your opponent's top hand and drop both of your elbows to pin your opponent's arms.

THRUSTING PRONGS - (front bear hug - arms pinned)

- simultaneously thrust both of your thumbs up and into your opponent's groin

BLUE BELT TECHNIQUES

SWINGING PENDULUM - (front right roundhouse kick)

- right inward block simultaneously with a left downward block (universal block)

OBSTRUCTING THE STORM - (front right step through overhead club)

- cross your right wrist over your left wrist (upward cross block) to block your opponent's attacking hand

SLEEPER - (front right step-through punch)

- right vertical punch to opponent's face with a right knee drop to your opponent's right rib cage

GIFT IN RETURN - (front hand shake)

- left hand assist your right hand, as well as your opponent's right hand, to strike to your opponent's groin

GREEN BELT TECHNIQUES

BEGGING HANDS - (front two-hand grab to wrists)

- twin torqueing heel palm thrusts under your opponent's ribcage

THRUSTING WEDGE - (front two-hand high push)

- thrusting the outer portion of both of your forearms forward and using them as a wedge against the inside of your opponent's arms

DEFYING THE STORM - (front right step-through roundhouse club)

- strike your opponent's right wrist with a left extended outward hand sword with a right inward hand sword to your opponent's right bicep.

REPEATED DEVASTATION - (full nelson)

- drive both of your elbows down to your opponent's biceps (palms facing you) as you straighten and stiffen your knees, body and neck.

CROSSED TWIGS - (rear two-hand grab to wrists)

- counter grab both of your opponent's wrists as you step pull forward and down
- execute two downward heel palm strikes to your opponent's left kidney and left ribcage

3rd DEGREE BROWN BELT TECHNIQUES

RETURNING STORM - (right roundhouse and backhand club attack)

- both of your arms strike vertically, so that your left forearm strikes at your opponent's right elbow joint and your right forearm strikes at your opponent's right wrist

Linear Master Key Moves

GLANCING SPEAR - (front right direct wrist grab to left arm)

- have your right hand (palm down) circle clockwise under your opponent's right hand and to the outside of your opponent's right wrist as you pivot into a left reverse bow and yanking him diagonally down past your right hip

GATHERING CLOUDS - (front right straight shuffle punch)

- right front scoop kick to your opponent's groin and a simultaneous counterclockwise right two-finger eye hook to your opponent's left eye

FALLEN CROSS - (rear two-hand choke)

- grab both of your opponent's wrists with both of your hands (right to right and left to left). Turn your head counterclockwise so your neck puts pressure against your opponent's left thumb and forces him to release his grab and possibly break his thumb joint.

DOMINATING CIRCLES - (front offset right hand grab to right shoulder)

- have your right hand assist in turning your opponent by applying a hammerlock on his right arm yank his right arm toward you to dislocate his shoulder. Your left hand assists your right hand

TWIST OF FATE - (front two-hand push)

- force your opponent's arms to loop forward, down and back toward you

BLINDING SACRIFICE - (front two-hand shoulder grab)

- thrust both of your forearms forward, thus using them as wedges inside of your opponent's arms
- two underhand heel palm strikes/squeezes to your opponent's groin.
- have the small fingers of both of your hands flick to your opponent's eyes followed by twin thumb scoops to his eyes.

SQUATTING SACRIFICE - (rear bear hug - arms free)

- both of your elbows strike down to your opponent's forearms

DESPERATE FALCONS - (front two-hand direct grabs to both wrists)

- left outward back knuckle strike to your opponent's face. Simultaneously deliver a right thrusting vertical punch to his right ribcage

2nd DEGREE BROWN BELT TECHNIQUES

CAPTURING THE STORM - (front right step-through overhead club)

- deliver a cross block (with your right wrist crossed over and on top of your left wrist) as it wedges against the right wrist of your opponent's attacking arm

TWIRLING SACRIFICE - (full nelson)

- have both of your arms grab the back of your opponent's knees and lift your opponent's legs off the ground

Linear Master Key Moves

KNEEL OF COMPULSION - (right flank, right step-through punch)

- both of your arms pull your opponent's shoulders back and down

MENACING TWIRL - (left hand rear belt grab)

- left knee kick to your opponent's groin. Counter balance this action by having your right hand now check high (across your opponent's chest)
- right knee kick to your opponent's groin. Counter balance this action by having your left hand now check high (across your opponent's chest)

BACKBREAKER - (right flank, right step-through punch)

- both of your arms pull your opponent's shoulders back and toward you
- two downward back knuckle strikes to the left and right humerus of the shoulders of your opponent

DECEPTIVE PANTHER - (combination right front snap kick (low) and right roundhouse kick (high)

- simultaneously deliver a left downward block to the inside of your opponent's right low kick and position a right inward block for his right high kick. (universal)

HEAVENLY ASCENT - (front two-hand choke, arms straight)

- execute two upward forearm strikes (which act as a wedge) to the inside of your opponent's forearms to break the choke.

DEFENSIVE CROSS - (front right front snap kick)

- execute a downward cross block (right hand over left hand) on your opponent's right ankle

BOWING TO BUDDHA - (front right roundhouse kick)

- right inward block with a left extended outward block to the inside of your opponent's right leg

1st DEGREE BROWN BELT TECHNIQUES

DANCE OF DARKNESS - (front right kick and right punch combination)

- execute a right outward back knuckle strike with a left vertical punch combination to your opponent's right kidney and right ribs

BEAR AND THE RAM - (front right punch / rear bear hug - arms free)

- simultaneously strike down with both of your elbows against the forearms of opponent

THRUST INTO DARKNESS - (rear right step-through punch)

- right outward back knuckle strike to your opponent's left temple. Simultaneous with the back-knuckle strike, deliver a left vertical punch to his spine.

LEAP OF DEATH - (front right step-through straight punch)

- land in a diamond stance so that the heels of both feet strike your opponent's kidneys

Linear Master Key Moves

- executing simultaneous heel palm strikes to the back of your opponent's mastoids
- concave stance as you pull up and toward you with both of your hand using your knees to brace down and against your opponent's shoulder blades.
- drop your left knee onto your opponent's upper spine. With this action simultaneously execute a left-hand push to the back of your opponent's head to again force his face to the ground

RAINING LANCE - (front right step-through overhead knife attack)

- your left hand assists your right in guiding and controlling the path of your opponent's weapon

UNFURLING CRANE - (front left and right punch)

- right knife-edge kick to the inside of your opponent's right knee as you execute a right inward hand sword to the left side of his neck.

FATAL CROSS - (front two-hand attempted low grab or push)

- two snapping uppercut punches to your opponent's floating ribs
- execute two, two-finger eye pokes
- left hand grabs opponent's left shoulder, right hand grabs his right shoulder as you jerk your opponent off balance

REVERSING CIRCLES - (front left roundhouse kick and left punch combination)

- execute a universal block (right downward with a left inward block) to the inside of his left leg.

- right knife-edge kick to the inside of your opponent's right thigh simultaneous with a right outward back knuckle strike to your opponent's left temple.

COURTING THE TIGER - (flank left and right arm and should grab / two men)

- grab the wrist of the opponent at your right flank (opponent #1) with your right hand to pull him off balance. Simultaneous with this action push (opponent #2) away from you with your left arm (anchoring your left elbow down and into his right ribs).

GATHERING OF THE SNAKES - (front left and rear right punch / two men)

- grab his shoulders (right hand to right shoulder and left hand to left shoulder). Deliver a right knife-edge kick to the back of opponent #1's left knee. As you kick, counter balance your kick by pulling your arms toward you.

DESTRUCTIVE FANS - (left flank right step-through punch)

- Execute a left front crossover toward 3 o'clock, in the process sweeping your opponent's right leg. Your left hand grabs and pulls your opponent's right arm

1st DEGREE BLACK BELT TECHNIQUES

DESTRUCTIVE KNEEL - (front right step-through punch)

- right outward back knuckle strike to your opponent's lower spine, simultaneous with a left vertical punch to his upper spine

THRUSTING LANCE - (front right step-through low knife thrust)

- right downward hammerfist to your opponent's mastoid. Simultaneous with these actions, deliver a left hammerfist to his right ribcage.

PRANCE OF THE TIGER - (right flank, right step-through uppercut punch)

- right knife-edge kick to the inside of your opponent's left knee. (The kick combination is actually a side chicken kick.) Simultaneous with your right kick, execute a right outward back knuckle strike to your opponent's right temple

FATAL DEVIATION - (front right and left punch combination)

- right hand circle clockwise, and diagonally down, to force your opponent's right arm against the right side of his body and hip. Simultaneously have your left hand circle clockwise and execute a left inward horizontal heel palm strike to the right side of your opponent's jaw.

SNAKES OF WISDOM - (flank left and right shoulder grabs / two men)

- circle your arms in the fashion of *Obscure Claws* as you now break your opponents' elbows

CIRCLING THE STORM - (front - right club thrust)

- right downward outward heel palm claw to the back and underside of your opponent's groin. While striking your opponent's groin from the back side have your left hand positionally check across your opponent's back
- your right hand drops to your opponent's back as a positional check against his arms. While dropping your right hand, have your left leg execute a left front crossover sweep to your opponent's right leg.

TWIRLING HAMMERS - (front left step-through punch)

- execute a right thrusting sweep kick to the shin of your opponent's right leg as you deliver a right thrusting vertical punch to your opponent's face while simultaneously delivering a left heel palm strike to the back of your opponent's head.

PIERCING LANCE - (front right low knife thrust while arms are up)

- your right hand grabs your opponent's right wrist as your left hand forms the shape of a crane and hooks onto the left side of your opponent's neck and throat. Pivot counterclockwise as your left forearm fulcrums on top of your opponent's right shoulder (using the back also) and forces your opponent's neck, throat, and head back.

Linear Master Key Moves

DEFYING THE ROD - (front right pistol)

- execute a right front snapping ball kick to your opponent's groin simultaneous with a right two-finger eye poke

ESCAPE FROM DARKNESS - (left rear flank right step-through punch)

- your right hand checks your opponent's right shoulder as you deliver a left vertical punch to the right side of your opponent's jaw

TWISTED ROD - (front right pistol)

- have your right knee drop down onto your opponent's throat. Simultaneous with this action execute a right two-finger eye poke to your opponent's eyes

Section 2

Circular Master Key Moves

The Circles

3.1

Repeating Circles

ORANGE BELT TECHNIQUES

REPEATING MACE - (front step through lunging left-hand push)

- left hand hooks (waiter's check) on top and to the outside of your opponent's left elbow, and deliver a right inward raking hammerfist to your opponent's left kidney.

PURPLE BELT TECHNIQUES

REVERSING MACE - (front left step through straight punch)

- right inward and left outward parry combination to the outside of your opponent's left punch. right inward parry continues to circle counterclockwise, and becomes a right outward back knuckle strike to your opponent's left lower rib cage

BLUE BELT TECHNIQUES

THUNDERING HAMMERS - (front right step through punch)

- strike to your opponent's left kidney with a left downward hammerfist as your right fist cocks near your right ear; left horizontal forearm check on top of your opponent's right shoulder; right downward hammerfist strike to the back of your opponent's neck.

GREEN BELT TECHNIQUES

DESTRUCTIVE TWINS - (two-hand choke - pull in)

- right inward block to the outside of your opponent's left arm and a left inside downward block (palm down) to the top of his right arm, converting it into a left vertical outward block outside of your opponent's left arm.

HUGGING PENDULUM - (front right drag-up thrusting sidekick)

- right outward horizontal back knuckle strike to your opponent's right mastoid followed by a left-hand check to his right shoulder

3rd DEGREE BROWN BELT TECHNIQUES

FLASHING MACE - (front right step through punch)

- strike to your opponent's right lower ribcage with a left outward horizontal back knuckle and have your right hand execute an inward heel palm bracing angle check to your opponent's right upper arm.
- Left upward hooking check (your left hand hooks like a waiter carrying a tray) on top of your opponent's right arm.

Have your right hand circle counterclockwise as you loop a right overhead back knuckle strike to your opponent's face or left temple.

GLANCING SPEAR - (front right direct wrist grab to left arm)

- left front crossover in the direction of 4:30 as you sweep your opponent's right leg; execute a right spinning stiff legged sweep to the back of your opponent's right leg toward 4:30

CIRCLING THE HORIZON - (front right step through punch)

- execute a left inward parry to the outside of your opponent's right arm; right hand circles clockwise tracking under your left wrist, and striking as a right thrusting vertical back knuckle to the right cheek bone of your opponent.

CIRCLING DESTRUCTION - (front left step through punch)

- right inward parry and left outward parry combination to the outside of your opponent's left arm; right outward back knuckle strike to your opponent's left lower ribcage

2nd DEGREE BROWN BELT TECHNIQUES

LEAP FROM DANGER - (rear two-hand push)

- deliver a right roundhouse kick to your opponent's solar plexus; left spinning back heel kick to your opponent's right ribs

Kenpo Karate Master Keys

ROTATING DESTRUCTION - (front right thrust & left spinning back kicks)

- left roundhouse kick to your opponent's head; right spinning hooking heel kick to your opponent's solar plexus

KNEEL OF COMPULSION - (right flank, right step through punch)

- double parry (left inward parry to the outside of your opponent's right wrist, followed by a right outward parry to the outside of your opponent's right elbow).

BACKBREAKER - (right flank, right step through punch)

- double parry (left inward parry to the outside of your opponent's right wrist, followed by a right outward parry to the opponent's right elbow.)

DEFENSIVE CROSS - (front right front snap kick)

- continue the clockwise direction of your orbiting hands to the left of your body as convert your right hand into an outward overhead back knuckle strike to the right side of your opponent's face, with your left hand trailing close behind. Have your right hand strike diagonally through your opponent's face as it travels down and past your right hip (palm facing 12 o'clock). With your left hand trailing close behind (following the same corresponding path) convert it into a left inward overhead heel palm strike to the right mastoid of your opponent

1st DEGREE BROWN BELT TECHNIQUES

CIRCLING FANS - (front left / right punch combination

- right inward downward diagonal parry to the top of your opponent's left arm; left inward downward diagonal parry to the top and outside of your opponent's right arm; right upper cut punch to your opponent's forehead

DANCE OF DARKNESS - (front right kick and right punch combination)

- double parry to the outside of his right arm (left inward parry at the wrist or forearm, followed by a right outward parry at or above the elbow); right outward back knuckle strike with a left vertical punch combination to your opponent's right kidney and right ribs
- left front crossover sweep (toward 4:30) to your opponent's right leg; pivot and execute a right leg sweep (again toward 4:30) and buckle the back of your opponent's right leg

PROTECTING FANS - (front left and right punch combination)

- left inward horizontal heel palm parry to the inside of your opponent's left punch; right extended outward block (done as a handsword) to the outside of your opponent's right arm.

UNFURLING CRANE - (front left and right punch)

- left outward block to the inside of your opponent's right punch. Be sure to precede this block with a right inward block as part of a Double Factor;

- left inward overhead claw to the bridge of your opponent's nose; right rolling back knuckle strike to your opponent's face

GATHERING OF THE SNAKES - (front left / rear-right punch / two men)

- right inward parry and left outward parry combination to the outside of your opponent's left arm; right outward back knuckle strike to your opponent's left lower ribcage

DESTRUCTIVE FANS - (left flank right step through punch)

- right outward/left inward parry combination to the outside of your opponent's right punch (right parry to his wrist and left parry to his elbow). Your right hand continues its clockwise circle and as your settle into your horse stance deliver a right hammerfist, palm up, to your opponent's solar plexus.
- left front crossover toward 3 o'clock, in the process sweeping your opponent's right leg; pivot and execute a right spinning stiff-leg sweep of your opponent's right leg

GLANCING LANCE - (front right shuffle knife thrust)

- right inward horizontal heel palm claw to your opponent's face; circle your left hand clockwise as you execute a left inward middle knuckle strike to your opponent's right mastoid; inward horizontal elbow strike to your opponent's ribs

1st DEGREE BLACK BELT TECHNIQUES

RAM AND THE EAGLE - (front right punch and rear left hand collar grab)

- right inward diagonal back knuckle rake to opponent #1's right cheek bone and temple; left outward horizontal back knuckle to
- ribs; right hand executes an inward heel palm detaining check to his right upper arm; right front snap ball kick

CIRCLING THE STORM - (front right club thrust)

- right downward outside palm out parry to the outside of the club and a left inward block to the outside of your opponent's right arm
- right horizontal inward elbow strike to your opponent's right lower ribcage; left outward elbow strike to your opponent's solar plexus; right inward heel palm claw to your opponent's face

ENTWINED LANCE - (front right step-through low knife thrust)

- right outward back knuckle strike to your opponent's right maxillary hinge; left inward hammerfist strike to the back of your opponent's neck

TWIRLING HAMMERS - (front left step through punch)

- left extended outward block to the outside of your opponent's left arm; right looping overhead back knuckle strike to your opponent's right mastoid

ESCAPE FROM DARKNESS - (left rear flank, right step-through punch)

- left outward claw across the face of your opponent; right inward downward diagonal hammerfist strike to the left side of your opponent's jaw.

3.2
Following Circles

ORANGE BELT TECHNIQUES

CRASHING WINGS - (rear bear hug - arms free)

- left outward elbow to your opponent's face followed by a right inward downward hammerfist to your opponent's bladder

PURPLE BELT TECHNIQUES

RAINING CLAW - (front right uppercut punch)

- right inward downward block, followed by a left inward overhead claw followed by a right vertical back knuckle thrust

SPIRALING TWIG - (rear bear hug - arms free)

- both of your hands continue to twist your opponent's right wrist clockwise in a very tight circle

TWIRLING WINGS - (rear stiff two-hand neck or shoulder grab)

- left vertical outward block followed by a right inward horizontal elbow strike

THRUSTING PRONGS - (front bear hug - arms pinned)

- your left hand circles over and on top of (clockwise) your opponent's right arm (forming the shape of a crane), and pins (with the assistance of your anchored left elbow) your opponent's right arm to you. Pull with your left arm as you rotate from your hips while simultaneously delivering a right inward horizontal elbow strike to the right side of your opponent's face or ribs

GREEN BELT TECHNIQUES

SHIELD AND MACE - (front right step through punch)

- strike the back of your opponent's right knee with a right handsword as your left hand circles clockwise to check just below your opponent's right shoulder

TRIPPING ARROW - (rear bear hug - arms free)

- left hand grab your opponent's left shoulder and pull it down as you execute a right hooking inward horizontal heel palm strike to your opponent's left jaw hinge

FLASHING WINGS - (front right step through punch)

- outward hooking hand sword to the back of your opponent's neck followed with a left inward hand sword strike to the back of your opponent's neck

WINGS OF SILK - (rear two-arm lock)

- standing naturally with your arms locked from the rear, stomp your opponent's left instep with your left foot as your left hand pinches the nerve located on the crest of your opponent's left hip.

- As your right arm starts to slip out of your opponent's right arm execute a right back obscure elbow strike to the underside of your opponent's chin "with" a simultaneous right back scoop heel kick to your opponent's groin.

3rd DEGREE BROWN BELT TECHNIQUES

OBSCURE CLAWS - (right flank left hand shoulder grab)

- right hand circles clockwise and claws (in an outward and upward manner) to your opponent's face. Follow up immediately with a left inward claw to your opponent's face.

DOMINATING CIRCLES - (front offset right hand grab to right shoulder)

- have your right foot circle clockwise into a horse stance planting it in back of and down on your opponent's right leg to buckle it. As you circle your right leg, circle a right outward overhead elbow strike. In Sync with the planting of your right foot have your elbow strike down and on top of your opponent's right forearm.

SQUATTING SACRIFICE - (rear bear hug - arms free)

- have both of your hands grab and pull up on your opponent's right ankle to force him on his back. twist your opponent's right ankle clockwise (pushing down on your opponent's toes with your left heel palm and pulling up on his ankle with the fingers and heel of your right hand.).

DESPERATE FALCONS - (front two-hand direct grabs to both wrists)

- circle both of your arms clockwise having them travel under, around, and over your opponent's right wrist

2nd DEGREE BROWN BELT TECHNIQUES

BROKEN GIFT - (front handshake)

- execute a left upward flapping elbow strike under the joint of your opponent's right elbow, while your right arm pulls down to cause an elbow break.

CAPTURING THE STORM - (front right step through overhead club

- grab your opponent's right wrist with both of your hands and guide your opponent's right arm down, in a clockwise motion, so that your opponent's club strikes against his right knee

TWIRLING SACRIFICE - (full nelson)

- lift your opponent's legs off the ground. Twirl counterclockwise (360 degrees) by first having your left foot step back toward 4:30. Continue your twirl and have your right foot step toward 6 o'clock, then your left foot toward 7:30

BACKBREAKER - (right flank, right step through punch)

- grab your opponent's chin with your right hand as your left hand moves to the right side of your opponent's head (the fingers of

- your left hand point to your left). Immediately twist your opponent's head clockwise (breaking your opponent's neck). execute two heel palm claws to your opponent's face.

DECEPTIVE PANTHER - (combination low right front snap kick and high right roundhouse kick)

- deliver a right downward back knuckle strike to your opponent's right mastoid followed by a left downward hammerfist to the right side of your opponent's neck.
- deliver a right stiff-arm lifting back knuckle strike to your opponent's face followed by a right back kick to his groin. This kick employs the grafting of thrusting and lifting methods of execution.

HEAVENLY ASCENT - (front two hand choke, arms straight)

- right downward back knuckle strike to your opponent's nose and face followed by a left heel palm claw strike to your opponent's nose and face

TAMING THE MACE - (front right step through punch with a wall behind you)

- with both of your hands grasping your opponent, keeping your arms in close to you, and with your elbows bent, have your left foot step back toward 4:30 into a right neutral bow (facing 10:30). Immediately pivot counterclockwise.

- right knee kick to your opponent's groin. Simultaneous with this action execute a right inward horizontal elbow strike to your opponent's throat

DEFENSIVE CROSS - (front right front snap kick)

- have your left hand convert into the shape of a crane (fingers and palm out) as it hooks inside of, and under your opponent's right foot. (Have your right hand remain on top of your opponent's right foot to act as a check.) Without disrupting the flow of your hands, guide your opponent's kicking leg diagonally down, and past your left hip.

BOWING TO BUDDHA - (front right roundhouse kick)

- right upward elbow strike to your opponent's groin. Your elbow strike should complete its Path of Travel as a positional right upward block with the right clenched palm facing you. Simultaneously with this positional block, execute a left upward heel palm strike to his groin
- slide your right hand over the top of the toes of your opponent's left foot, as your left hand grabs (traveling over and on top of) the outer portion of the left heel of his foot. Pivot counterclockwise into a right reverse bow (facing 1 o'clock). Through the proper use of body momentum coupled with the fulcrum, flip your opponent onto his stomach

Circular Master Key Moves

GLANCING WING - (front left uppercut punch)

- hook your left hand down and out (clockwise) outside of your opponent's left arm as you deliver a right chopping punch to your opponent's left ribcage

1st DEGREE BROWN BELT TECHNICUES

BEAR AND THE RAM - (front right punch/rear bear hug - arms free)

- left outward elbow to your opponent's face followed by a right inward downward hammerfist to your opponent's bladder

PARTING OF THE SNAKES - (front right punch / rear attempt)

- duck under the right punch of your front opponent; execute a left upward claw to his face, simultaneous with a right underhand reverse hand sword to his groin.

LEAP OF DEATH - (front right step-through straight punch)

- pulling up and against your opponent's chin with your right hand and pushing down on the back of your opponent's head with your left hand to snap his neck

RAINING LANCE - (front right step-through overhead knife attack)

- left hooking wrist (shape of a crane) whereby your left forearm utilizes your opponent's right shoulder as a fulcrum. This fulcrum coordinated with the momentum of your body will force your opponent over your right knee. Deliver a right downward diagonal hammerfist to your opponent's heart

UNFURLING CRANE - (front left and right punch)

- strike under his jaw with a right obscure elbow. Continue your Path of Travel and transform it into an upward five-finger claw to your opponent's face. Follow this with a right front scoop kick to his groin.

FATAL CROSS - (front two-hand attempted low grab or push)

- have your left hand, which is still grabbing your opponent's left shoulder, turn your opponent clockwise so that his back is toward you. Simultaneous with this action have your right hand release your opponent's right shoulder and speedily convert it into a right inward elbow strike to the left side of his jaw.

REVERSING CIRCLES - (front left roundhouse kick & left punch combo)

- your right hand assists your left hand (which is holding on to your opponent's left wrist) in grabbing your opponent's left hand in a wrist lock. Manipulate both of your hands, twist your opponent's left wrist clockwise.

GLANCING LANCE - (front right shuffle knife thrust)

- your right arm circles counterclockwise as you execute a right outside downward parry. This parry hooks on the outside of your opponent's right elbow. As you parry, deliver a left inward horizontal heel palm strike to the outside of your opponent's right shoulder.

1st DEGREE BLACK BELT TECHNIQUES

DESTRUCTIVE KNEEL - (front right step-through punch)

- left outward back knuckle strike to your opponent's right lower ribcage simultaneous with a right inward heel palm claw across your opponent's face

THRUSTING LANCE - (front right step-through low knife thrust)

- control Manipulate your opponent's right arm with a lock and twist

CAPTURING THE ROD - (front right pistol against your chest)

- both your hands twist your opponent's wrist and pistol clockwise

PIERCING LANCE - (front right low knife thrust while arms are up)

- executing a right hooking downward parry to the outside of your opponent's right wrist. As your right parry directs the knife wielding hand toward 4:30 execute a left heel palm parry to the outside of your opponent's right elbow
- simultaneously having both of your hands twist and force your opponent's knife into his own throat

ESCAPE FROM DARKNESS - (left rear flank right step-through punch)

- have your right hand grab under your opponent's jaw. As you pull your right hand, execute a left heel palm strike to your opponent's right mastoid (as in Leap of Death). The simultaneous pull and strike are for the purpose of snapping your opponent's neck.

TWISTED ROD - (front right pistol)

- right outward hooking parry (like a waiter carrying a tray) to the outside and on top of your opponent's right hand at the pistol while simultaneously having your left hand reach and grab the top of your opponent's right hand at the pistol.
- have your right forearm (now perpendicular to your opponent's right arm) strike, pin and press against the back of your opponent's right hand. During this action pull in with your left hand (which acts as a fulcrum) and push forward with your right forearm (opposing force) in forcing your opponent's right hand and barrel of the pistol to point toward his face.
- left hand and right forearm assist each other in twisting your opponent's right wrist counterclockwise in order to break his wrist.

3.3

Spreading Circles

ORANGE BELT TECHNIQUES

FIVE SWORDS - (front right step through roundhouse punch)

- left outward handsword strike to the left side of your opponent's neck while your right hand is a positional check against any potential danger from your opponent's left arm.

EVADING THE STORM - (front right step through overhead club attack)

- right extended outward block as you have your left hand positionally check close to your left rib

PURPLE BELT TECHNIQUES

CALMING THE STORM - (front right step through roundhouse club)

- right outward back knuckle strike to your opponent's right lower ribs a left upward hooking parry on top of your opponent's right arm

BLUE BELT TECHNIQUES

PARTING WINGS - (front two-hand push)

- two extended outward handswords to the inside of your opponent's wrists

SHIELD AND SWORD - (front left step through punch)

- left extended outward block to the outside of your opponent's left elbow. Have your right handsword cock beside your right ear, palm out

CHARGING RAM - (front tackle with your opponent's arms extended)

- simultaneously redirect your opponent's left arm down and out with a right outside downward parry, and execute a left outward heel palm parry to the left side of your opponent's head

HOOKING WINGS - (front two-hand low push)

- hook with both of your hands (shape of a crane) to the inside of your opponent's wrists, jerking your opponent's arms down, outside and past your hips.

GREEN BELT TECHNIQUES

BEGGING HANDS - (front two-hand grab to wrists)

- simultaneously have both of your hands circle (from inside out) up, over and on top of your opponent's wrists

THRUSTING WEDGE - (front two-hand high push)

- two rolling upward-outward claws to your opponent's eyes.

3rd DEGREE BROWN BELT TECHNIQUES

DETOUR FROM DOOM - (front right roundhouse kick)

- right back knuckle strike to your opponent's stomach as your left hand hooks downward on the back of your opponent's neck

TWIST OF FATE - (front two-hand push)

- both of your hands execute extended outward handswords to the inside of your opponent's wrists

BLINDING SACRIFICE - (front two-hand shoulder grab)

- two rolling upward-outward claws (your right hand rolls counterclockwise and your left clockwise) to your opponent's eyes.
- two vertical outward blocks as positional checks.

BROKEN RAM - (front tackle with your opponent's arms wide)

- right outside downward parry to the inside of your opponent's left arm, as your left hand checks the inside of your opponent's head or neck.

2nd DEGREE BROWN BELT TECHNIQUES

CIRCLES OF PROTECTION - (front right step through overhead punch)

- right upward parry as you deliver a left upward ripping claw to your opponent's face

GLANCING WING - (front left uppercut punch)

- left hand hooks to the back of your opponent's neck, thus forcing your opponent to bend forward. Simultaneously have your right hand check your opponent's left arm to his body

1st DEGREE BROWN BELT TECHNIQUES

FATAL CROSS - (front two-hand attempted low grab or push)

- hook the inside of both of your opponent's wrists. Without any loss of action jerk your opponent's arms toward you as they travel outside, down, and past your hips

1st DEGREE BLACK BELT TECHNIQUES

MARRIAGE OF THE RAMS - (flank right and left shoulder grabs from close in)

- execute two underhand back knuckle strikes to the groin of each of your opponents

- grab and jerk both of your opponents' ankles up and slightly out so that both legs are then pulled out from under them

RAM AND THE EAGLE - (front right punch and rear left hand collar grab)

- left outward handsword strikes to the left side of your opponent's neck. Your right hand acts as a positional check against any potential danger from your opponent's left arm.

PRANCE OF THE TIGER - (right flank, right step-through uppercut punch)

- left outside downward, hooking parry to the inside of your opponent's right elbow simultaneous with a right ascending forearm check.

SNAKES OF WISDOM - (flank left & right shoulder grabs / two men)

- circle both of your arms in the fashion of *Obscure Claws* to first claw your opponents' face
- outward back knuckle strike to the ribcage of each opponent (right back knuckle strike to the left ribcage of opponent #1, and left back knuckle strike to the right ribcage
- grab their ankles and jerk them out from under your opponents (pulling toward you)

3.4

Closing Circles

ORANGE BELT TECHNIQUES

LOCKING HORNS - (Front headlock)

- inward horizontal elbow strike with a simultaneous heel palm strike to jaw (sandwich)

GRIP OF DEATH - (Left flank right arm headlock)

- hammer fist to opponent's groin with a hammer fist to opponent's kidney

PURPLE BELT TECHNIQUES

LEAPING CRANE - (Front right step through punch)

- inward parry with a middle knuckle strike

SNAPPING TWIG - (Front left-hand chest push)

- inward horizontal elbow strike with an inward horizontal heelpalm strike (sandwich)

CROSSING TALON - (Front right cross wrist grab)

- downward heelpalm strike to back of head with knee strike to face (sandwich)

SPIRALING TWIG - (rear bear hug - arms free)

- right and left middle knuckle fists strike to back of opponent's hand

LOCKED WING - (rear hammerlock)

- knee strike to your opponent's check synchronized with an inward overhead heelpalm strike

BLUE BELT TECHNIQUES

SHIELD AND SWORD - (front left step through punch)

- inward horizontal elbow strike to lower ribcage with Bracing Angle Check of the arm
- waiters check down and out on arm with inward raking hammerfist strike to kidney

SLEEPER - (front right step through punch)

- inward block at or above the outside of opponent's elbow with inner diagonal wrist strike to neck
- grab opposite hand (from behind opponent's head) and pull toward you, applying pressure to his neck

CIRCLING WING - (rear two-hand choke - arms bent)

- upward elbow strike to chin with a downward sliding check to opponent's shoulder

GREEN BELT TECHNIQUES

SHIELD AND MACE - (front right step through punch)

- downward hammerfist strike to top of kidney with a Bracing Angle Check to elbow
- hand pins opponent's arm down as opposite hand circles striking opponent's face and eyes

RAKING MACE - (front two-hand lapel grab - pulling in)

- inward horizontal elbow strike to side of jaw with a heelpalm strike to opposite side of jaw (sandwich)

DESTRUCTIVE TWINS - (two hand choke - pulling in)

- overhead punch to opponent's face with a uppercut punch to groin to stomach)

FLASHING WINGS - (front right step through punch)

- inward checking block with inward horizontal elbow strike to ribcage
- outward elbow strike to kidney with outward heelpalm strike to face

HUGGING PENDULUM - (front right drag-up thrusting sidekick)

- cross one hand to opposite hip and positionally check with other hand ("hug")

REPEATED DEVASTATION - (full nelson)

- strike over and back of your head with both of your fists to your opponent's face

3rd DEGREE BROWN BELT TECHNIQUES

GATHERING CLOUDS - (front right straight shuffle punch)

- inward parry to outside of arm with an inward vertical middle-knuckle rake through his ribcage

BRUSHING THE STORM - (right flank, right step through overhead club)

- left inward parry to the outside of opponent's arm while striking opponent's jaw with a heel palm thrust

OBSCURE CLAWS - (right flank left hand shoulder grab)

- looping inward backknuckle strike to opponent's mastoid with an inward horizontal heel palm thrust

DOMINATING CIRCLES - (front offset right hand grab to right shoulder)

- hook around outside opponent's neck while other hand assists turning him by applying a hammerlock to arm.

BLINDING SACRIFICE - (front two-hand shoulder grab)

- two inward hooking backnuckle strikes to the back of opponent's kidneys
- two inverted backnuckle strikes to opponent's temples
- with both of your elbows raised drop them down and in toward each other thus striking and sandwiching your opponent's jaw hinges
- both hands grab the back of opponent's head and, with anchored elbows push his head down into a right knee strike to face

2nd DEGREE BROWN BELT TECHNIQUES

CIRCLES OF PROTECTION - (front right step through overhead punch)

- left hand circles counterclockwise forcing opponent's arm down to right side of body while right arm circles clockwise and executes a underhand heel palm claw to groin.

ESCAPE FROM DEATH - (right rear arm choke)

- hammerfist strike to groin with hammerfist strike to kidney

KNEEL OF COMPULSION - (right flank, right step through punch)

- inward horizontal elbow to right side of head with inward horizontal heelpalm strike to head (sandwich)

Circular Master Key Moves

INTERCEPTING THE RAM - (front tackle)

- knee kick to opponent's solar plexus with an inward overhead hammerfist to kidney (sandwich)

CROSS OF DEATH - (front two-hand cross choke)

- extended outward hooking parry to outside of elbow with a chopping punch to opponent's kidney

TAMING THE MACE - (front right step through punch with a wall behind you)

- inward parry on the outside of opponent's punch with inward handsword to the inside of opponent's bicep
- check and grab opponent's hand at the wrist while grabbing and pulling down his shoulder

DEFENSIVE CROSS - (front right front snap kick)

- grab and pull opponent's hair with a front snap ball kick to groin
- maintain one hand grab while executing a upward lifting stiff-arm backnuckle to face (sandwich)

BOWING TO BUDDHA - (front right roundhouse kick)

- grab and pull testicles toward you while delivering a downward backnuckle strike to sandwich

1st DEGREE BROWN BELT TECHNIQUES

FATAL CROSS - (front two-hand attempted low grab or push)

- (crossed arms) two snapping outward backnuckle strikes to opponent's temples (scissors)

CIRCLING WINDMILLS - (front - two-hand push followed by a right-hand punch)

- windmill left hand counterclockwise as you claw up, slightly out and to your opponent's face with a clockwise right inward hammerfist to floating ribs
- upward parry to expose the side of body with an inward hammerfist to floating ribs

1st DEGREE BLACK BELT TECHNIQUES

MARRIAGE OF THE RAMS - (flank right and left shoulder grabs from close in)

- your arms hook over and on top of your opponents' shoulders as you proceed to pinch their arms with both of yours. As you settle into your right neutral bow, unite both of your arms (right over left) and force your opponents" heads to collide.

ESCAPE FROM THE STORM - (right flank, right overhead club attack)

- inward parry to the outside of your opponent's arm while striking to your opponent's jaw with a heel palm thrust

Circular Master Key Moves

CAPTURING THE ROD - (front right pistol against your chest)

- outward parry (to deflect the barrel of the pistol) while simultaneously grabbing the pistol

PRANCE OF THE TIGER - (right flank, right step-through uppercut punch)

- knee kick to your opponent's solar plexus simultaneous with an inward overhead hammerfist strike
- inward overhead hammerfist strike down to the back of his head simultaneous with a knee kick

FATAL DEVIATION - (front right and left punch combination)

- heel palm bracing against your opponent's jaw as opposite arm circles with inward horizontal elbow strike to the other side of jaw

SNAKES OF WISDOM - (flank left and right shoulder grabs / two men)

- circle both of your hands back, around, and on top of their heads of each opponent and smash your hands together.

CIRCLING THE STORM - (front right club thrust)

- strike your opponent's face with an inward heel palm claw while your left hand positionally checks

TWIRLING HAMMERS - (front left step through punch)

- right pressing check at your opponent's left elbow while simultaneously pivoting into a right forward bow and delivering a

- left inward horizontal elbow strike to your opponent's left lower ribcage
- thrusting vertical punch to your opponent's face while simultaneously delivering a heel palm strike to the back of your opponent's head.

DEFYING THE ROD - (front - right pistol)

- simultaneously execute a right front knee kick to your opponent's sternum and an inward overhead hammering strike with the butt of the pistol to the back of your opponent's spine (sandwich)

3.5
Reversing Circles

YELLOW BELT TECHNIQUES

THE GRASP OF DEATH - (side headlock)

- grab your opponent's right wrist with your right hand while grabbing your opponent's right inner thigh with your left hand and pinching the flesh of that leg; release the grip of your left hand and have your left foot step forward toward 10:30 into a left neutral bow stance as you simultaneously strike the back of your opponent's right elbow with your left forearm while pulling his wrist in and toward you with your right hand (arm bar)

3rd DEGREE BROWN BELT TECHNIQUES

GIFT OF DESTINY - (front handshake)

- have your left hand grab your opponent's right wrist. Your palm and fingers are on top of his wrist joint. Have your right hand circle counterclockwise *contouring* your opponent's right fingers with the palm of your right hand. (Your fingers are now pointing up and your thumb is down.) During this action your left hand still controls your opponent's right wrist. Immediately have your

- right hand grab your opponent's fingers. While stepping back toward 6 o'clock into a left neutral bow (facing 12 o'clock) turn your right hand clockwise, twisting your opponent's wrist palm up. Simultaneously turn your left hand counterclockwise (as your left heel of palm uses your opponent right wrist as a PIVOT POINT) ending with your left hand (palm up) controlling under his right wrist (which is also palm up). At the completion of your right hand twist reach further around your opponent's right wrist with your left hand, this allows you to twist your opponent's wrist even further.

2nd DEGREE BROWN BELT TECHNIQUES

BROKEN GIFT - (front handshake)

- from the right handshake have your left hand grab opponent's wrist. have your left hand assist by grabbing your opponent's right wrist as both of your hands twist your opponent's right wrist and arm clockwise, violently jerking his arm diagonally down past your left hip.

1st DEGREE BROWN BELT TECHNIQUES

RAINING LANCE - (front right step-through overhead knife attack)

- with your left hand pressing the knife against his thigh, have your left hand convert into a palm up "tiger's mouth "". Have your left

Circular Master Key Moves

- arm *track* up your opponent's right arm, pressing against it, on its
- way to choking your opponent's Adam's Apple. Your right hand switches places, palm down, to continue pressing and checking the knife into your opponent's thigh. Switch both of your hands so that your left forearm now presses your opponent's right arm, as your left hand grabs and squeezes your opponent's testicles. Simultaneously have your right hand circle counterclockwise in the shape of a crab hand pinch (palm facing your opponent). Have the crab hand pinch hook and pinch your opponent's eyes.

UNFURLING CRANE - (front left & right punch)

- right outward block, right inward block, then right hammerfist to your opponent's groin as your arm guards inside your opponent's left arm (waiter's check) and is positionally checked for opponent's possible right arm follow up strike. Left inward overhead claw to the bridge of your opponent's nose. Reverse the path of your right hammerfist, and execute a right rolling back knuckle strike to your opponent's face

CIRCLING WINDMILLS - (front two-hand push followed by a right-hand punch)

- have your right hand circle clockwise in a windmill fashion. As it travels up and under your opponent's right arm it transitionally converts into a right upward parry to expose the right side of your opponent's body. Simultaneous with this parry, execute a left (counterclockwise) inward hammerfist to his right floating ribs.

- Now have your left hand reverse its circle (clockwise) and check your opponent's right arm down and diagonally toward his body while simultaneously delivering a right inward hammerfist strike diagonally down and across the bridge of your opponent's nose

REVERSING CIRCLES - (front left roundhouse kick & left punch combo)

- as your opponent attempts to punch your head with his left hand, pivot into a right forward bow (facing 12 o'clock) while executing a right upward block under, as well as inside of, his left attacking arm. Simultaneous with your right block deliver a left thrusting heel palm (fingers pointing toward 3 o'clock) to his left floating ribs. Pivot into a right neutral bow as you reverse the motion of your left hand and convert it into a left upward block under your opponent's left arm. Simultaneous with this action reverse the motion of your right arm and convert it into a right thrusting heel palm strike (fingers pointing toward 9 o'clock) to his right floating ribs.

1st DEGREE BLACK BELT TECHNIQUES

TWIRLING HAMMERS - (front left step through punch)

- have your right hand perform a right pressing check at your opponent's left elbow. This is simultaneously done while pivoting into a right forward bow and delivering a left inward horizontal elbow strike to your opponent's left lower ribcage. Without any loss of motion convert your left elbow strike into an upward hooking wrist check (hooking over his left arm at his elbow like a waiter carrying a tray). Simultaneous with this action pivot into a right neutral bow as you now loop (clockwise) a right inward hammerfist strike, diagonally and down, to your opponent's right kidney.

End Note

Statements made in this document are solely my opinions. They are based on the understanding that I have developed during my years learning, teaching and practicing Kenpo Karate.

My hope is this work will enhance other students understanding of Kenpo. If the reader disagrees with something, I would encourage them to work out why they disagree to better understand their own personal art. Kenpo Karate is all about learning.

Circular Master Key Moves

Kenpo Karate is a martial art that is marked by continuous learning. There is always more to know.

With that in mind, this document will never be finished.

Doug Parent

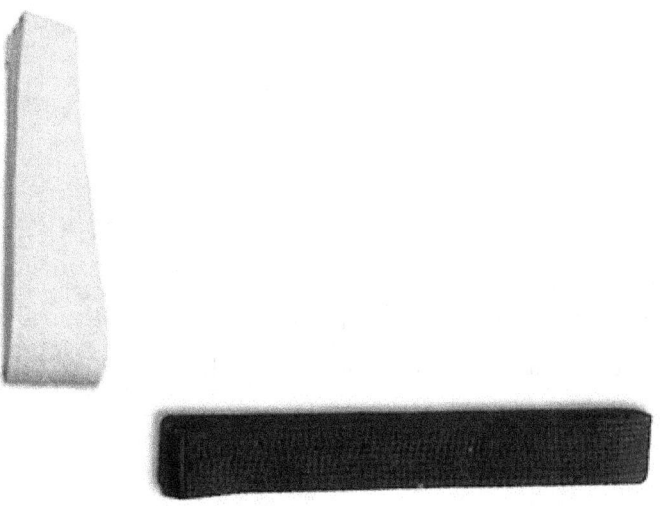

Index by Self Defense Technique

ALTERNATING MACES	yellow	Singular
ATTACKING MACE	yellow	Alternating Lines
ATTACKING MACE	yellow	Opposing Lines
BACKBREAKER	2nd Brown	Following Circles
BACKBREAKER	2nd Brown	Repeating Circles
BACKBREAKER	2nd Brown	Twin Lines
BEAR AND THE RAM	1st Brown	Following Circles
BEAR AND THE RAM	1st Brown	Parting Lines
BEAR AND THE RAM	1st Brown	Twin Lines
BEGGING HANDS	green	Alternating Lines
BEGGING HANDS	green	Spreading Circles
BEGGING HANDS	green	Twin Lines
BLINDING SACRIFICE	3rd Brown	Closing Circles
BLINDING SACRIFICE	3rd Brown	Spreading Circles
BLINDING SACRIFICE	3rd Brown	Twin Lines
BOW OF COMPULSION	blue	Singular
BOWING TO BUDDHA	2nd Brown	Twin Lines
BOWING TO BUDDHA	2nd Brown	Closing Circles
BOWING TO BUDDHA	2nd Brown	Crossing Lines
BOWING TO BUDDHA	2nd Brown	Following Circles
BOWING TO BUDDHA	2nd Brown	Opposing Lines
BROKEN GIFT	2nd Brown	Following Circles
BROKEN GIFT	2nd Brown	Opposing Lines
BROKEN GIFT	2nd Brown	Reversing Circles
BROKEN GIFT	2nd Brown	Singular
BROKEN RAM	3rd Brown	Crossing Lines
BROKEN RAM	3rd Brown	Parting Lines
BROKEN RAM	3rd Brown	Spreading Circles

Index by Self Defense Technique

BROKEN ROD	1st Black	Opposing Lines
BROKEN ROD	1st Black	Singular
BRUSHING THE STORM	3rd Brown	Closing Circles
BRUSHING THE STORM	3rd Brown	Opposing Lines
BRUSHING THE STORM	3rd Brown	Singular
BUCKLING BRANCH	purple	Alternating Lines
CALMING THE STORM	purple	Crossing Lines
CALMING THE STORM	purple	Parting Lines
CALMING THE STORM	purple	Spreading Circles
CAPTURED LEAVES	purple	Opposing Lines
CAPTURED TWIGS	yellow	Singular
CAPTURING THE ROD	1st Black	Closing Circles
CAPTURING THE ROD	1st Black	Following Circles
CAPTURING THE ROD	1st Black	Opposing Lines
CAPTURING THE ROD	1st Black	Parting Lines
CAPTURING THE ROD	1st Black	Singular
CAPTURING THE STORM	2nd Brown	Crossing Lines
CAPTURING THE STORM	2nd Brown	Following Circles
CAPTURING THE STORM	2nd Brown	Twin Lines
CHARGING RAM	blue	Alternating Lines
CHARGING RAM	blue	Spreading Circles
CIRCLE OF DOOM	3rd Brown	Singular
CIRCLES OF PROTECTION	2nd Brown	Closing Circles
CIRCLES OF PROTECTION	2nd Brown	Opposing Lines
CIRCLES OF PROTECTION	2nd Brown	Spreading Circles
CIRCLING DESTRUCTION	3rd Brown	Alternating Lines
CIRCLING DESTRUCTION	3rd Brown	Opposing Lines
CIRCLING DESTRUCTION	3rd Brown	Repeating Circles
CIRCLING FANS	1st Brown	Alternating Lines
CIRCLING FANS	1st Brown	Repeating Circles
CIRCLING THE HORIZON	3rd Brown	Repeating Circles
CIRCLING THE HORIZON	3rd Brown	Singular

Kenpo Karate Master Keys

CIRCLING THE STORM	1st Black	Closing Circles
CIRCLING THE STORM	1st Black	Crossing Lines
CIRCLING THE STORM	1st Black	Opposing Lines
CIRCLING THE STORM	1st Black	Repeating Circles
CIRCLING THE STORM	1st Black	Twin Lines
CIRCLING WINDMILLS	1st Brown	Closing Circles
CIRCLING WINDMILLS	1st Brown	Opposing Lines
CIRCLING WINDMILLS	1st Brown	Parting Lines
CIRCLING WINDMILLS	1st Brown	Reversing Circles
CIRCLING WING	blue	Closing Circles
CIRCLING WING	blue	Opposing Lines
CLIPPING THE STORM	1st Brown	Alternating Lines
CLUTCHING FEATHERS	orange	Alternating Lines
CLUTCHING FEATHERS	orange	Opposing Lines
CONQUERING SHIELD	green	Crossing Lines
CONQUERING SHIELD	green	Singular
COURTING THE TIGER	1st Brown	Alternating Lines
COURTING THE TIGER	1st Brown	Twin Lines
CRASHING WINGS	orange	Following Circles
CRASHING WINGS	orange	Twin Lines
CROSS OF DEATH	2nd Brown	Closing Circles
CROSS OF DEATH	2nd Brown	Opposing Lines
CROSS OF DESTRUCTION	blue	Crossing Lines
CROSSED TWIGS	green	Twin Lines
CROSSING TALON	purple	Closing Circles
CROSSING TALON	purple	Crossing Lines
CRUSHING HAMMER	purple	Singular
CRUSHING HAMMER	purple	Opposing Lines
DANCE OF DARKNESS	1st Brown	Alternating Lines
DANCE OF DARKNESS	1st Brown	Opposing Lines
DANCE OF DARKNESS	1st Brown	Repeating Circles
DANCE OF DARKNESS	1st Brown	Twin Lines

Index by Self Defense Technique

DANCE OF DEATH	orange	Opposing Lines
DARTING MACE	blue	Alternating Lines
DARTING MACE	blue	Opposing Lines
DECEPTIVE PANTHER	2nd Brown	Following Circles
DECEPTIVE PANTHER	2nd Brown	Twin Lines
DEFENSIVE CROSS	2nd Brown	Closing Circles
DEFENSIVE CROSS	2nd Brown	Following Circles
DEFENSIVE CROSS	2nd Brown	Repeating Circles
DEFENSIVE CROSS	2nd Brown	Twin Lines
DEFLECTING HAMMER	yellow	Singular
DEFYING THE ROD	1st Black	Closing Circles
DEFYING THE ROD	1st Black	Opposing Lines
DEFYING THE ROD	1st Black	Singular
DEFYING THE ROD	1st Black	Twin Lines
DEFYING THE STORM	green	Opposing Lines
DEFYING THE STORM	green	Twin Lines
DELAYED SWORD	yellow	Singular
DESPERATE FALCONS	3rd Brown	Following Circles
DESPERATE FALCONS	3rd Brown	Singular
DESPERATE FALCONS	3rd Brown	Twin Lines
DESTRUCTIVE FANS	1st Brown	Opposing Lines
DESTRUCTIVE FANS	1st Brown	Repeating Circles
DESTRUCTIVE FANS	1st Brown	Twin Lines
DESTRUCTIVE KNEEL	1st Black	Crossing Lines
DESTRUCTIVE KNEEL	1st Black	Following Circles
DESTRUCTIVE KNEEL	1st Black	Opposing Lines
DESTRUCTIVE KNEEL	1st Black	Twin Lines
DESTRUCTIVE TWINS	green	Closing Circles
DESTRUCTIVE TWINS	green	Opposing Lines
DESTRUCTIVE TWINS	green	Repeating Circles
DETOUR FROM DOOM	3rd Brown	Alternating Lines
DETOUR FROM DOOM	3rd Brown	Parting Lines

Kenpo Karate Master Keys

DETOUR FROM DOOM	3rd Brown	Spreading Circles
DOMINATING CIRCLES	3rd Brown	Closing Circles
DOMINATING CIRCLES	3rd Brown	Following Circles
DOMINATING CIRCLES	3rd Brown	Opposing Lines
DOMINATING CIRCLES	3rd Brown	Twin Lines
ENCOUNTER WITH DANGER	3rd Brown	Alternating Lines
ENTANGLED WING	green	Crossing Lines
ENTWINED LANCE	1st Black	Opposing Lines
ENTWINED LANCE	1st Black	Parting Lines
ENTWINED LANCE	1st Black	Repeating Circles
ENTWINED LANCE	1st Black	Singular
ENTWINED MACES	1st Black	Opposing Lines
ENTWINED MACES	1st Black	Parting Lines
ENTWINED MACES	1st Black	Singular
ESCAPE FROM DARKNESS	1st Black	Following Circles
ESCAPE FROM DARKNESS	1st Black	Repeating Circles
ESCAPE FROM DARKNESS	1st Black	Twin Lines
ESCAPE FROM DEATH	2nd Brown	Alternating Lines
ESCAPE FROM DEATH	2nd Brown	Closing Circles
ESCAPE FROM DEATH	2nd Brown	Parting Lines
ESCAPE FROM THE STORM	1st Black	Closing Circles
ESCAPE FROM THE STORM	1st Black	Crossing Lines
ESCAPE FROM THE STORM	1st Black	Opposing Lines
ESCAPE FROM THE STORM	1st Black	Singular
EVADING THE STORM	orange	Alternating Lines
EVADING THE STORM	orange	Opposing Lines
EVADING THE STORM	orange	Spreading Circles
FALCONS OF FORCE	1st Brown	Opposing Lines
FALLEN CROSS	3rd Brown	Crossing Lines
FALLEN CROSS	3rd Brown	Twin Lines

Index by Self Defense Technique

FALLING FALCON	2nd Brown	Crossing Lines
FALLING FALCON	2nd Brown	Opposing Lines
FATAL CROSS	1st Brown	Alternating Lines
FATAL CROSS	1st Brown	Closing Circles
FATAL CROSS	1st Brown	Following Circles
FATAL CROSS	1st Brown	Spreading Circles
FATAL CROSS	1st Brown	Twin Lines
FATAL DEVIATION	1st Black	Closing Circles
FATAL DEVIATION	1st Black	Parting Lines
FATAL DEVIATION	1st Black	Singular
FATAL DEVIATION	1st Black	Twin Lines
FIVE SWORDS	orange	Alternating Lines
FIVE SWORDS	orange	Spreading Circles
FIVE SWORDS	orange	Twin Lines
FLASHING MACE	3rd Brown	Repeating Circles
FLASHING WINGS	green	Closing Circles
FLASHING WINGS	green	Following Circles
FLASHING WINGS	green	Parting Lines
FLIGHT TO FREEDOM	blue	Crossing Lines
FLIGHT TO FREEDOM	blue	Opposing Lines
GATHERING CLOUDS	3rd Brown	Closing Circles
GATHERING CLOUDS	3rd Brown	Twin Lines
GATHERING OF THE SNAKES	1st Brown	Alternating Lines
GATHERING OF THE SNAKES	1st Brown	Opposing Lines
GATHERING OF THE SNAKES	1st Brown	Repeating Circles
GATHERING OF THE SNAKES	1st Brown	Twin Lines
GIFT IN RETURN	blue	Opposing Lines
GIFT IN RETURN	blue	Twin Lines
GIFT OF DESTINY	3rd Brown	Crossing Lines
GIFT OF DESTINY	3rd Brown	Reversing Circles

Kenpo Karate Master Keys

GIFT OF DESTRUCTION	orange	Crossing Lines
GIFT OF DESTRUCTION	orange	Opposing Lines
GLANCING LANCE	1st Brown	Repeating Circles
GLANCING LANCE	1st Brown	Alternating Lines
GLANCING LANCE	1st Brown	Crossing Lines
GLANCING LANCE	1st Brown	Following Circles
GLANCING SALUTE	orange	Crossing Lines
GLANCING SALUTE	orange	Opposing Lines
GLANCING SPEAR	3rd Brown	Alternating Lines
GLANCING SPEAR	3rd Brown	Repeating Circles
GLANCING SPEAR	3rd Brown	Twin Lines
GLANCING WING	2nd Brown	Crossing Lines
GLANCING WING	2nd Brown	Following Circles
GLANCING WING	2nd Brown	Spreading Circles
GRASPING EAGLES	1st Brown	Parting Lines
GRIP OF DEATH	orange	Closing Circles
GRIPPING TALON	3rd Brown	Opposing Lines
GRIPPING TALON	3rd Brown	Parting Lines
GRIPPING TALON	3rd Brown	Singular
HEAVENLY ASCENT	2nd Brown	Following Circles
HEAVENLY ASCENT	2nd Brown	Opposing Lines
HEAVENLY ASCENT	2nd Brown	Twin Lines
HOOKING WINGS	blue	Singular
HOOKING WINGS	blue	Spreading Circles
HUGGING PENDULUM	green	Closing Circles
HUGGING PENDULUM	green	Repeating Circles
INTERCEPTING THE RAM	2nd Brown	Closing Circles
KNEEL OF COMPULSION	2nd Brown	Closing Circles
KNEEL OF COMPULSION	2nd Brown	Repeating Circles
KNEEL OF COMPULSION	2nd Brown	Twin Lines
LEAP FROM DANGER	2nd Brown	Repeating Circles
LEAP OF DEATH	1st Brown	Crossing Lines

Index by Self Defense Technique

Technique	Belt	Category
LEAP OF DEATH	1st Brown	Following Circles
LEAP OF DEATH	1st Brown	Opposing Lines
LEAP OF DEATH	1st Brown	Twin Lines
LEAPING CRANE	purple	Alternating Lines
LEAPING CRANE	purple	Closing Circles
LOCKED WING	purple	Closing Circles
LOCKED WING	purple	Crossing Lines
LOCKED WING	purple	Opposing Lines
LOCKING HORNS	orange	Closing Circles
LOCKING HORNS	orange	Parting Lines
LONE KIMONO	orange	Crossing Lines
LONE KIMONO	orange	Singular
MACE OF AGGRESSION	yellow	Singular
MACE OF AGGRESSION	yellow	Opposing Lines
MARRIAGE OF THE RAMS	1st Black	Closing Circles
MARRIAGE OF THE RAMS	1st Black	Spreading Circles
MENACING TWIRL	2nd Brown	Parting Lines
MENACING TWIRL	2nd Brown	Twin Lines
OBSCURE CLAWS	3rd Brown	Crossing Lines
OBSCURE CLAWS	3rd Brown	Following Circles
OBSCURE SWORD	purple	Alternating Lines
OBSCURE WING	purple	Opposing Lines
OBSTRUCTING THE STORM	blue	Crossing Lines
OBSTRUCTING THE STORM	blue	Opposing Lines
OBSTRUCTING THE STORM	blue	Twin Lines
PARTING OF THE SNAKES	1st Brown	Alternating Lines
PARTING OF THE SNAKES	1st Brown	Following Circles
PARTING OF THE SNAKES	1st Brown	Parting Lines
PARTING WINGS	blue	Alternating Lines
PARTING WINGS	blue	Spreading Circles

Kenpo Karate Master Keys

PIERCING LANCE	1st Black	Crossing Lines
PIERCING LANCE	1st Black	Following Circles
PIERCING LANCE	1st Black	Opposing Lines
PIERCING LANCE	1st Black	Parting Lines
PIERCING LANCE	1st Black	Twin Lines
PRANCE OF THE TIGER	1st Black	Closing Circles
PRANCE OF THE TIGER	1st Black	Spreading Circles
PRANCE OF THE TIGER	1st Black	Twin Lines
PROTECTING FANS	1st Brown	Opposing Lines
PROTECTING FANS	1st Brown	Repeating Circles
RAINING CLAW	purple	Following Circles
RAINING LANCE	1st Brown	Following Circles
RAINING LANCE	1st Brown	Reversing Circles
RAINING LANCE	1st Brown	Twin Lines
RAKING MACE	green	Closing Circles
RAKING MACE	green	Opposing Lines
RAM AND THE EAGLE	1st Black	Alternating Lines
RAM AND THE EAGLE	1st Black	Parting Lines
RAM AND THE EAGLE	1st Black	Repeating Circles
RAM AND THE EAGLE	1st Black	Spreading Circles
REPEATED DEVASTATION	green	Closing Circles
REPEATED DEVASTATION	green	Opposing Lines
REPEATED DEVASTATION	green	Twin Lines
REPEATING MACE	orange	Repeating Circles
REPEATING MACE	orange	Singular
REPRIMANDING THE	1st Black	Alternating Lines
REPRIMANDING THE BEARS	1st Black	Opposing Lines
REPRIMANDING THE BEARS	1st Black	Parting Lines
RETREATING PENDULUM	green	Singular

Index by Self Defense Technique

RETURNING STORM	3rd Brown	Alternating Lines
RETURNING STORM	3rd Brown	Crossing Lines
RETURNING STORM	3rd Brown	Twin Lines
REVERSING CIRCLES	1st Brown	Crossing Lines
REVERSING CIRCLES	1st Brown	Following Circles
REVERSING CIRCLES	1st Brown	Parting Lines
REVERSING CIRCLES	1st Brown	Reversing Circles
REVERSING CIRCLES	1st Brown	Twin Lines
REVERSING MACE	purple	Repeating Circles
ROTATING DESTRUCTION	2nd Brown	Repeating Circles
SCRAPING HOOF	orange	Twin Lines
SECURING THE STORM	2nd Brown	Crossing Lines
SECURING THE STORM	2nd Brown	Opposing Lines
SECURING THE STORM	2nd Brown	Parting Lines
SHIELD AND MACE	green	Closing Circles
SHIELD AND MACE	green	Following Circles
SHIELD AND MACE	green	Parting Lines
SHIELD AND SWORD	blue	Closing Circles
SHIELD AND SWORD	blue	Spreading Circles
SHIELDING HAMMER	orange	Singular
SLEEPER	blue	Closing Circles
SLEEPER	blue	Twin Lines
SNAKES OF WISDOM	1st Black	Closing Circles
SNAKES OF WISDOM	1st Black	Spreading Circles
SNAKES OF WISDOM	1st Black	Twin Lines
SNAKING TALON	green	Opposing Lines
SNAKING TALON	green	Singular
SNAPPING TWIG	purple	Closing Circles
SNAPPING TWIG	purple	Crossing Lines
SNAPPING TWIG	purple	Opposing Lines
SPIRALING TWIG	purple	Closing Circles
SPIRALING TWIG	purple	Following Circles

Kenpo Karate Master Keys

SPIRALING TWIG	purple	Opposing Lines
SPIRALING TWIG	purple	Twin Lines
SQUATTING SACRIFICE	3rd Brown	Crossing Lines
SQUATTING SACRIFICE	3rd Brown	Following Circles
SQUATTING SACRIFICE	3rd Brown	Opposing Lines
SQUATTING SACRIFICE	3rd Brown	Twin Lines
SQUEEZING THE PEACH	blue	Parting Lines
STRIKING SERPENT'S HEAD	orange	Alternating Lines
STRIKING SERPENT'S HEAD	orange	Singular
SWINGING PENDULUM	blue	Twin Lines
SWORD AND HAMMER	yellow	Opposing Lines
SWORD AND HAMMER	yellow	Singular
SWORD OF DESTRUCTION	yellow	Singular
TAMING THE MACE	2nd Brown	Closing Circles
TAMING THE MACE	2nd Brown	Following Circles
TAMING THE MACE	2nd Brown	Opposing Lines
THE GRASP OF DEATH	yellow	Crossing Lines
THE GRASP OF DEATH	yellow	Reversing Circles
THRUST INTO DARKNESS	1st Brown	Alternating Lines
THRUST INTO DARKNESS	1st Brown	Twin Lines
THRUSTING LANCE	1st Black	Alternating Lines
THRUSTING LANCE	1st Black	Crossing Lines
THRUSTING LANCE	1st Black	Following Circles
THRUSTING LANCE	1st Black	Opposing Lines
THRUSTING LANCE	1st Black	Singular
THRUSTING LANCE	1st Black	Twin Lines
THRUSTING PRONGS	purple	Following Circles
THRUSTING PRONGS	purple	Twin Lines
THRUSTING SALUTE	orange	Alternating Lines
THRUSTING WEDGE	green	Opposing Lines
THRUSTING WEDGE	green	Spreading Circles

Index by Self Defense Technique

THRUSTING WEDGE	green	Twin Lines
THUNDERING HAMMERS	blue	Alternating Lines
THUNDERING HAMMERS	blue	Repeating Circles
TRIGGERED SALUTE	orange	Opposing Lines
TRIGGERED SALUTE	orange	Singular
TRIPPING ARROW	green	Following Circles
TRIPPING ARROW	green	Opposing Lines
TWIN KIMONO	blue	Crossing Lines
TWIRLING HAMMERS	1st Black	Closing Circles
TWIRLING HAMMERS	1st Black	Repeating Circles
TWIRLING HAMMERS	1st Black	Reversing Circles
TWIRLING HAMMERS	1st Black	Twin Lines
TWIRLING SACRIFICE	2nd Brown	Following Circles
TWIRLING SACRIFICE	2nd Brown	Twin Lines
TWIRLING WINGS	purple	Following Circles
TWIST OF FATE	3rd Brown	Crossing Lines
TWIST OF FATE	3rd Brown	Spreading Circles
TWIST OF FATE	3rd Brown	Twin Lines
TWISTED ROD	1st Black	Following Circles
TWISTED ROD	1st Black	Twin Lines
TWISTED TWIG	purple	Parting Lines
TWISTED TWIG	purple	Singular
UNFOLDING THE DARK	1st Black	Parting Lines
UNFURLING	1st Brown	Reversing Circles
UNFURLING CRANE	1st Brown	Following Circles
UNFURLING CRANE	1st Brown	Parting Lines
UNFURLING CRANE	1st Brown	Repeating Circles

Kenpo Karate Master Keys

UNFURLING CRANE	1st Brown	Twin Lines
UNWINDING PENDULUM	1st Brown	Parting Lines
WINGS OF SILK	green	Crossing Lines
WINGS OF SILK	green	Following Circles

Index by Self Defense Technique

Index by Belt Level

ALTERNATING MACES	yellow	Singular
ATTACKING MACE	yellow	Alternating Lines
ATTACKING MACE	yellow	Opposing Lines
CAPTURED TWIGS	yellow	Singular
DEFLECTING HAMMER	yellow	Singular
DELAYED SWORD	yellow	Singular
MACE OF AGGRESSION	yellow	Singular
MACE OF AGGRESSION	yellow	Opposing Lines
SWORD AND HAMMER	yellow	Opposing Lines
SWORD AND HAMMER	yellow	Singular
SWORD OF DESTRUCTION	yellow	Singular
THE GRASP OF DEATH	yellow	Crossing Lines
THE GRASP OF DEATH	yellow	Reversing Circles
CLUTCHING FEATHERS	orange	Alternating Lines
CLUTCHING FEATHERS	orange	Opposing Lines
CRASHING WINGS	orange	Following Circles
CRASHING WINGS	orange	Twin Lines
DANCE OF DEATH	orange	Opposing Lines
EVADING THE STORM	orange	Alternating Lines
EVADING THE STORM	orange	Opposing Lines
EVADING THE STORM	orange	Spreading Circles
FIVE SWORDS	orange	Alternating Lines
FIVE SWORDS	orange	Spreading Circles
FIVE SWORDS	orange	Twin Lines
GIFT OF DESTRUCTION	orange	Crossing Lines
GIFT OF DESTRUCTION	orange	Opposing Lines
GLANCING SALUTE	orange	Crossing Lines
GLANCING SALUTE	orange	Opposing Lines

Index by Belt Level

GRIP OF DEATH	orange	Closing Circles
LOCKING HORNS	orange	Closing Circles
LOCKING HORNS	orange	Parting Lines
LONE KIMONO	orange	Crossing Lines
LONE KIMONO	orange	Singular
REPEATING MACE	orange	Repeating Circles
REPEATING MACE	orange	Singular
SCRAPING HOOF	orange	Twin Lines
SHIELDING HAMMER	orange	Singular
STRIKING SERPENT'S HEAD	orange	Alternating Lines
STRIKING SERPENT'S HEAD	orange	Singular
THRUSTING SALUTE	orange	Alternating Lines
TRIGGERED SALUTE	orange	Opposing Lines
TRIGGERED SALUTE	orange	Singular
BUCKLING BRANCH	purple	Alternating Lines
CALMING THE STORM	purple	Crossing Lines
CALMING THE STORM	purple	Parting Lines
CALMING THE STORM	purple	Spreading Circles
CAPTURED LEAVES	purple	Opposing Lines
CROSSING TALON	purple	Closing Circles
CROSSING TALON	purple	Crossing Lines
CRUSHING HAMMER	purple	Singular
CRUSHING HAMMER	purple	Opposing Lines
LEAPING CRANE	purple	Alternating Lines
LEAPING CRANE	purple	Closing Circles
LOCKED WING	purple	Closing Circles
LOCKED WING	purple	Crossing Lines
LOCKED WING	purple	Opposing Lines
OBSCURE SWORD	purple	Alternating Lines
OBSCURE WING	purple	Opposing Lines
RAINING CLAW	purple	Following Circles
REVERSING MACE	purple	Repeating Circles

Kenpo Karate Master Keys

SNAPPING TWIG	purple	Closing Circles
SNAPPING TWIG	purple	Crossing Lines
SNAPPING TWIG	purple	Opposing Lines
SPIRALING TWIG	purple	Closing Circles
SPIRALING TWIG	purple	Following Circles
SPIRALING TWIG	purple	Opposing Lines
SPIRALING TWIG	purple	Twin Lines
THRUSTING PRONGS	purple	Following Circles
THRUSTING PRONGS	purple	Twin Lines
TWIRLING WINGS	purple	Following Circles
TWISTED TWIG	purple	Parting Lines
TWISTED TWIG	purple	Singular
BOW OF COMPULSION	blue	Singular
CHARGING RAM	blue	Alternating Lines
CHARGING RAM	blue	Spreading Circles
CIRCLING WING	blue	Closing Circles
CIRCLING WING	blue	Opposing Lines
CROSS OF DESTRUCTION	blue	Crossing Lines
DARTING MACE	blue	Alternating Lines
DARTING MACE	blue	Opposing Lines
FLIGHT TO FREEDOM	blue	Crossing Lines
FLIGHT TO FREEDOM	blue	Opposing Lines
GIFT IN RETURN	blue	Opposing Lines
GIFT IN RETURN	blue	Twin Lines
HOOKING WINGS	blue	Singular
HOOKING WINGS	blue	Spreading Circles
OBSTRUCTING THE STORM	blue	Crossing Lines
OBSTRUCTING THE STORM	blue	Opposing Lines
OBSTRUCTING THE STORM	blue	Twin Lines
PARTING WINGS	blue	Alternating Lines
PARTING WINGS	blue	Spreading Circles
SHIELD AND SWORD	blue	Closing Circles

Index by Belt Level

SHIELD AND SWORD	blue	Spreading Circles
SLEEPER	blue	Closing Circles
SLEEPER	blue	Twin Lines
SQUEEZING THE PEACH	blue	Parting Lines
SWINGING PENDULUM	blue	Twin Lines
THUNDERING HAMMERS	blue	Alternating Lines
THUNDERING HAMMERS	blue	Repeating Circles
TWIN KIMONO	blue	Crossing Lines
BEGGING HANDS	green	Alternating Lines
BEGGING HANDS	green	Spreading Circles
BEGGING HANDS	green	Twin Lines
CONQUERING SHIELD	green	Crossing Lines
CONQUERING SHIELD	green	Singular
CROSSED TWIGS	green	Twin Lines
DEFYING THE STORM	green	Opposing Lines
DEFYING THE STORM	green	Twin Lines
DESTRUCTIVE TWINS	green	Closing Circles
DESTRUCTIVE TWINS	green	Opposing Lines
DESTRUCTIVE TWINS	green	Repeating Circles
ENTANGLED WING	green	Crossing Lines
FLASHING WINGS	green	Closing Circles
FLASHING WINGS	green	Following Circles
FLASHING WINGS	green	Parting Lines
HUGGING PENDULUM	green	Closing Circles
HUGGING PENDULUM	green	Repeating Circles
RAKING MACE	green	Closing Circles
RAKING MACE	green	Opposing Lines
REPEATED DEVASTATION	green	Closing Circles
REPEATED DEVASTATION	green	Opposing Lines
REPEATED DEVASTATION	green	Twin Lines
RETREATING PENDULUM	green	Singular
SHIELD AND MACE	green	Closing Circles

Kenpo Karate Master Keys

SHIELD AND MACE	green	Following Circles
SHIELD AND MACE	green	Parting Lines
SNAKING TALON	green	Opposing Lines
SNAKING TALON	green	Singular
THRUSTING WEDGE	green	Opposing Lines
THRUSTING WEDGE	green	Spreading Circles
THRUSTING WEDGE	green	Twin Lines
TRIPPING ARROW	green	Following Circles
TRIPPING ARROW	green	Opposing Lines
WINGS OF SILK	green	Crossing Lines
WINGS OF SILK	green	Following Circles
BLINDING SACRIFICE	3rd Brown	Closing Circles
BLINDING SACRIFICE	3rd Brown	Spreading Circles
BLINDING SACRIFICE	3rd Brown	Twin Lines
BROKEN RAM	3rd Brown	Crossing Lines
BROKEN RAM	3rd Brown	Parting Lines
BROKEN RAM	3rd Brown	Spreading Circles
BRUSHING THE STORM	3rd Brown	Closing Circles
BRUSHING THE STORM	3rd Brown	Opposing Lines
BRUSHING THE STORM	3rd Brown	Singular
CIRCLE OF DOOM	3rd Brown	Singular
CIRCLING DESTRUCTION	3rd Brown	Alternating Lines
CIRCLING DESTRUCTION	3rd Brown	Opposing Lines
CIRCLING DESTRUCTION	3rd Brown	Repeating Circles
CIRCLING THE HORIZON	3rd Brown	Repeating Circles
CIRCLING THE HORIZON	3rd Brown	Singular
DESPERATE FALCONS	3rd Brown	Following Circles
DESPERATE FALCONS	3rd Brown	Singular
DESPERATE FALCONS	3rd Brown	Twin Lines
DETOUR FROM DOOM	3rd Brown	Alternating Lines
DETOUR FROM DOOM	3rd Brown	Parting Lines
DETOUR FROM DOOM	3rd Brown	Spreading Circles

Index by Belt Level

DOMINATING CIRCLES	3rd Brown	Closing Circles
DOMINATING CIRCLES	3rd Brown	Following Circles
DOMINATING CIRCLES	3rd Brown	Opposing Lines
DOMINATING CIRCLES	3rd Brown	Twin Lines
ENCOUNTER WITH DANGER	3rd Brown	Alternating Lines
FALLEN CROSS	3rd Brown	Crossing Lines
FALLEN CROSS	3rd Brown	Twin Lines
FLASHING MACE	3rd Brown	Repeating Circles
GATHERING CLOUDS	3rd Brown	Closing Circles
GATHERING CLOUDS	3rd Brown	Twin Lines
GIFT OF DESTINY	3rd Brown	Crossing Lines
GIFT OF DESTINY	3rd Brown	Reversing Circles
GLANCING SPEAR	3rd Brown	Alternating Lines
GLANCING SPEAR	3rd Brown	Repeating Circles
GLANCING SPEAR	3rd Brown	Twin Lines
GRIPPING TALON	3rd Brown	Opposing Lines
GRIPPING TALON	3rd Brown	Parting Lines
GRIPPING TALON	3rd Brown	Singular
OBSCURE CLAWS	3rd Brown	Crossing Lines
OBSCURE CLAWS	3rd Brown	Following Circles
RETURNING STORM	3rd Brown	Alternating Lines
RETURNING STORM	3rd Brown	Crossing Lines
RETURNING STORM	3rd Brown	Twin Lines
SQUATTING SACRIFICE	3rd Brown	Crossing Lines
SQUATTING SACRIFICE	3rd Brown	Following Circles
SQUATTING SACRIFICE	3rd Brown	Opposing Lines
SQUATTING SACRIFICE	3rd Brown	Twin Lines
TWIST OF FATE	3rd Brown	Crossing Lines
TWIST OF FATE	3rd Brown	Spreading Circles
TWIST OF FATE	3rd Brown	Twin Lines
BACKBREAKER	2nd Brown	Following Circles
BACKBREAKER	2nd Brown	Repeating Circles

Kenpo Karate Master Keys

BACKBREAKER	2nd Brown	Twin Lines
BOWING TO BUDDHA	2nd Brown	Twin Lines
BOWING TO BUDDHA	2nd Brown	Closing Circles
BOWING TO BUDDHA	2nd Brown	Crossing Lines
BOWING TO BUDDHA	2nd Brown	Following Circles
BOWING TO BUDDHA	2nd Brown	Opposing Lines
BROKEN GIFT	2nd Brown	Following Circles
BROKEN GIFT	2nd Brown	Opposing Lines
BROKEN GIFT	2nd Brown	Reversing Circles
BROKEN GIFT	2nd Brown	Singular
CAPTURING THE STORM	2nd Brown	Crossing Lines
CAPTURING THE STORM	2nd Brown	Following Circles
CAPTURING THE STORM	2nd Brown	Twin Lines
CIRCLES OF PROTECTION	2nd Brown	Closing Circles
CIRCLES OF PROTECTION	2nd Brown	Opposing Lines
CIRCLES OF PROTECTION	2nd Brown	Spreading Circles
CROSS OF DEATH	2nd Brown	Closing Circles
CROSS OF DEATH	2nd Brown	Opposing Lines
DECEPTIVE PANTHER	2nd Brown	Following Circles
DECEPTIVE PANTHER	2nd Brown	Twin Lines
DEFENSIVE CROSS	2nd Brown	Closing Circles
DEFENSIVE CROSS	2nd Brown	Following Circles
DEFENSIVE CROSS	2nd Brown	Repeating Circles
DEFENSIVE CROSS	2nd Brown	Twin Lines
ESCAPE FROM DEATH	2nd Brown	Alternating Lines
ESCAPE FROM DEATH	2nd Brown	Closing Circles
ESCAPE FROM DEATH	2nd Brown	Parting Lines
FALLING FALCON	2nd Brown	Crossing Lines
FALLING FALCON	2nd Brown	Opposing Lines
GLANCING WING	2nd Brown	Crossing Lines
GLANCING WING	2nd Brown	Following Circles
GLANCING WING	2nd Brown	Spreading Circles

Index by Belt Level

HEAVENLY ASCENT	2nd Brown	Following Circles
HEAVENLY ASCENT	2nd Brown	Opposing Lines
HEAVENLY ASCENT	2nd Brown	Twin Lines
INTERCEPTING THE RAM	2nd Brown	Closing Circles
KNEEL OF COMPULSION	2nd Brown	Closing Circles
KNEEL OF COMPULSION	2nd Brown	Repeating Circles
KNEEL OF COMPULSION	2nd Brown	Twin Lines
LEAP FROM DANGER	2nd Brown	Repeating Circles
MENACING TWIRL	2nd Brown	Parting Lines
MENACING TWIRL	2nd Brown	Twin Lines
ROTATING DESTRUCTION	2nd Brown	Repeating Circles
SECURING THE STORM	2nd Brown	Crossing Lines
SECURING THE STORM	2nd Brown	Opposing Lines
SECURING THE STORM	2nd Brown	Parting Lines
TAMING THE MACE	2nd Brown	Closing Circles
TAMING THE MACE	2nd Brown	Following Circles
TAMING THE MACE	2nd Brown	Opposing Lines
TWIRLING SACRIFICE	2nd Brown	Following Circles
TWIRLING SACRIFICE	2nd Brown	Twin Lines
BEAR AND THE RAM	1st Brown	Following Circles
BEAR AND THE RAM	1st Brown	Parting Lines
BEAR AND THE RAM	1st Brown	Twin Lines
CIRCLING FANS	1st Brown	Alternating Lines
CIRCLING FANS	1st Brown	Repeating Circles
CIRCLING WINDMILLS	1st Brown	Closing Circles
CIRCLING WINDMILLS	1st Brown	Opposing Lines
CIRCLING WINDMILLS	1st Brown	Parting Lines
CIRCLING WINDMILLS	1st Brown	Reversing Circles
CLIPPING THE STORM	1st Brown	Alternating Lines
COURTING THE TIGER	1st Brown	Alternating Lines
COURTING THE TIGER	1st Brown	Twin Lines
DANCE OF DARKNESS	1st Brown	Alternating Lines

Kenpo Karate Master Keys

DANCE OF DARKNESS	1st Brown	Opposing Lines
DANCE OF DARKNESS	1st Brown	Repeating Circles
DANCE OF DARKNESS	1st Brown	Twin Lines
DESTRUCTIVE FANS	1st Brown	Opposing Lines
DESTRUCTIVE FANS	1st Brown	Repeating Circles
DESTRUCTIVE FANS	1st Brown	Twin Lines
FALCONS OF FORCE	1st Brown	Opposing Lines
FATAL CROSS	1st Brown	Alternating Lines
FATAL CROSS	1st Brown	Closing Circles
FATAL CROSS	1st Brown	Following Circles
FATAL CROSS	1st Brown	Spreading Circles
FATAL CROSS	1st Brown	Twin Lines
GATHERING OF THE SNAKES	1st Brown	Alternating Lines
GATHERING OF THE SNAKES	1st Brown	Opposing Lines
GATHERING OF THE SNAKES	1st Brown	Repeating Circles
GATHERING OF THE SNAKES	1st Brown	Twin Lines
GLANCING LANCE	1st Brown	Repeating Circles
GLANCING LANCE	1st Brown	Alternating Lines
GLANCING LANCE	1st Brown	Crossing Lines
GLANCING LANCE	1st Brown	Following Circles
GRASPING EAGLES	1st Brown	Parting Lines
LEAP OF DEATH	1st Brown	Crossing Lines
LEAP OF DEATH	1st Brown	Following Circles
LEAP OF DEATH	1st Brown	Opposing Lines
LEAP OF DEATH	1st Brown	Twin Lines
PARTING OF THE SNAKES	1st Brown	Alternating Lines
PARTING OF THE SNAKES	1st Brown	Following Circles
PARTING OF THE SNAKES	1st Brown	Parting Lines
PROTECTING FANS	1st Brown	Opposing Lines
PROTECTING FANS	1st Brown	Repeating Circles

Index by Belt Level

RAINING LANCE	1st Brown	Following Circles
RAINING LANCE	1st Brown	Reversing Circles
RAINING LANCE	1st Brown	Twin Lines
REVERSING CIRCLES	1st Brown	Crossing Lines
REVERSING CIRCLES	1st Brown	Following Circles
REVERSING CIRCLES	1st Brown	Parting Lines
REVERSING CIRCLES	1st Brown	Reversing Circles
REVERSING CIRCLES	1st Brown	Twin Lines
THRUST INTO DARKNESS	1st Brown	Alternating Lines
THRUST INTO DARKNESS	1st Brown	Twin Lines
UNFURLING	1st Brown	Reversing Circles
UNFURLING CRANE	1st Brown	Following Circles
UNFURLING CRANE	1st Brown	Parting Lines
UNFURLING CRANE	1st Brown	Repeating Circles
UNFURLING CRANE	1st Brown	Twin Lines
UNWINDING PENDULUM	1st Brown	Parting Lines
BROKEN ROD	1st Black	Opposing Lines
BROKEN ROD	1st Black	Singular
CAPTURING THE ROD	1st Black	Closing Circles
CAPTURING THE ROD	1st Black	Following Circles
CAPTURING THE ROD	1st Black	Opposing Lines
CAPTURING THE ROD	1st Black	Parting Lines
CAPTURING THE ROD	1st Black	Singular
CIRCLING THE STORM	1st Black	Closing Circles
CIRCLING THE STORM	1st Black	Crossing Lines
CIRCLING THE STORM	1st Black	Opposing Lines
CIRCLING THE STORM	1st Black	Repeating Circles
CIRCLING THE STORM	1st Black	Twin Lines
DEFYING THE ROD	1st Black	Closing Circles
DEFYING THE ROD	1st Black	Opposing Lines
DEFYING THE ROD	1st Black	Singular
DEFYING THE ROD	1st Black	Twin Lines

Kenpo Karate Master Keys

DESTRUCTIVE KNEEL	1st Black	Crossing Lines
DESTRUCTIVE KNEEL	1st Black	Following Circles
DESTRUCTIVE KNEEL	1st Black	Opposing Lines
DESTRUCTIVE KNEEL	1st Black	Twin Lines
ENTWINED LANCE	1st Black	Opposing Lines
ENTWINED LANCE	1st Black	Parting Lines
ENTWINED LANCE	1st Black	Repeating Circles
ENTWINED LANCE	1st Black	Singular
ENTWINED MACES	1st Black	Opposing Lines
ENTWINED MACES	1st Black	Parting Lines
ENTWINED MACES	1st Black	Singular
ESCAPE FROM DARKNESS	1st Black	Following Circles
ESCAPE FROM DARKNESS	1st Black	Repeating Circles
ESCAPE FROM DARKNESS	1st Black	Twin Lines
ESCAPE FROM THE STORM	1st Black	Closing Circles
ESCAPE FROM THE STORM	1st Black	Crossing Lines
ESCAPE FROM THE STORM	1st Black	Opposing Lines
ESCAPE FROM THE STORM	1st Black	Singular
FATAL DEVIATION	1st Black	Closing Circles
FATAL DEVIATION	1st Black	Parting Lines
FATAL DEVIATION	1st Black	Singular
FATAL DEVIATION	1st Black	Twin Lines
MARRIAGE OF THE RAMS	1st Black	Closing Circles
MARRIAGE OF THE RAMS	1st Black	Spreading Circles
PIERCING LANCE	1st Black	Crossing Lines
PIERCING LANCE	1st Black	Following Circles
PIERCING LANCE	1st Black	Opposing Lines
PIERCING LANCE	1st Black	Parting Lines
PIERCING LANCE	1st Black	Twin Lines
PRANCE OF THE TIGER	1st Black	Closing Circles
PRANCE OF THE TIGER	1st Black	Spreading Circles
PRANCE OF THE TIGER	1st Black	Twin Lines

Index by Belt Level

RAM AND THE EAGLE	1st Black	Alternating Lines
RAM AND THE EAGLE	1st Black	Parting Lines
RAM AND THE EAGLE	1st Black	Repeating Circles
RAM AND THE EAGLE	1st Black	Spreading Circles
REPRIMANDING THE BEARS	1st Black	Alternating Lines
REPRIMANDING THE BEARS	1st Black	Opposing Lines
REPRIMANDING THE BEARS	1st Black	Parting Lines
SNAKES OF WISDOM	1st Black	Closing Circles
SNAKES OF WISDOM	1st Black	Spreading Circles
SNAKES OF WISDOM	1st Black	Twin Lines
THRUSTING LANCE	1st Black	Alternating Lines
THRUSTING LANCE	1st Black	Crossing Lines
THRUSTING LANCE	1st Black	Following Circles
THRUSTING LANCE	1st Black	Opposing Lines
THRUSTING LANCE	1st Black	Singular
THRUSTING LANCE	1st Black	Twin Lines
TWIRLING HAMMERS	1st Black	Closing Circles
TWIRLING HAMMERS	1st Black	Repeating Circles
TWIRLING HAMMERS	1st Black	Reversing Circles
TWIRLING HAMMERS	1st Black	Twin Lines
TWISTED ROD	1st Black	Following Circles
TWISTED ROD	1st Black	Twin Lines
UNFOLDING THE DARK	1st Black	Parting Lines

***** ***** *****

www.ingramcontent.com/pod-product-compliance
Lightning Source LLC
Chambersburg PA
CBHW071504080526
44587CB00014B/2209